Juan Gris

Head of a Man—Self-portrait, 1916 (cat. 42)

Juan Gris

Mark Rosenthal

University Art Museum
University of California, Berkeley

Abbeville Press · Publishers · New York

Library of Congress Cataloguing in Publication Data

Gris, Juan, 1887–1927.
  Juan Gris: University Art Museum,
University of California, Berkeley.

  Bibliography: p.
  Includes index.
  1. Gris, Juan, 1887–1927—Exhibitions.
I. Rosenthal, Mark. II. University of
California, Berkeley. University Art
Museum. III. Title.
N7113.G83A4 1983 759.6 83–6060
ISBN 0-89659-400-9
ISBN 0-89659-401-7 (pbk.)

First edition

Published on the occasion of the exhibition *Juan Gris*, organized
by University Art Museum, University of California, Berkeley.
Exhibition shown at the National Gallery of Art, Washington, D.C.
(October 16–December 31, 1983); University Art Museum, Berkeley
(February 1–April 8, 1984); and The Solomon R. Guggenheim Museum,
New York (May 18–July 15, 1984).

Major funding for this exhibition was provided by the National
Endowment for the Arts, a Federal agency; the Paul L. and
Phyllis Wattis Foundation; and the University Art Museum Council.
The exhibition is supported with an indemnity provided by the
Federal Council for the Arts and the Humanities.

Full citations for works in the exhibition can be found in the
Catalogue of the Exhibition. Works illustrated but not a part
of the exhibition are indicated as figures.

Front cover:
38 *Guitar on a Table*, 1915

Back cover:
6 *Portrait of Picasso*, 1912

Editor:
Ann Karlstrom

Designer:
Nathan Garland

14R-5c

Contents

Foreword

Considerable rewards await the viewer who spends time with a picture by Juan Gris. Therein is an art of high refinement and, surprisingly, some mystery. These ostensibly formal investigations comprise, as well, a certain preoccupation with the evocative power of objects. That quality together with the brilliant range of color and an extraordinary subtlety of composition mark Gris's unique achievement within the Cubist pantheon. Now, for the first time in America in twenty-five years, the breadth of Gris's achievement can be surveyed in an exhibition.

A project of this scale requires extraordinary commitments, not the least of which must be made by the owners of the works of art. To these individuals and to the trustees and staffs of the institutional lenders, we express our profound gratitude. By their generosity, understanding of the art of Juan Gris is greatly enhanced.

I want to express my appreciation to J. Carter Brown, Director, National Gallery of Art; and Thomas M. Messer, Director, The Solomon R. Guggenheim Museum. Their participation and cooperation contributed enormously to the organization of the exhibition.

Mark Rosenthal skillfully organized all aspects of the exhibition, from the selection of works to the writing of the catalogue.

We are grateful to Georges Gonzalez-Gris, the artist's son, for graciously extending permission to reproduce his father's work. Douglas Cooper very generously provided important advice. The exhibition has been aided substantially by the efforts of Louise Leiris, for which we are deeply grateful.

We are honored to acknowledge the patronage of the Ambassador of France to the United States, M. Bernard Vernier-Palliez; the Cultural Counselor of the French Embassy to the United States, Jean-Marie Guehenno; and the Association Française d'Action Artistique. We are equally delighted that the exhibition has been distinguished by the high patronage of the Ambassador of Spain to the United States, Sr. Gabriel Mañueco.

The exhibition could not have occurred without the generous financial support of the National Endowment for the Arts, a Federal agency; The Paul L. and Phyllis Wattis Foundation; and the University Art Museum Council. We are also appreciative of the support of the Federal Council on the Arts and the Humanities, through the offices of the National Endowment for the Arts, for indemnifying many of the foreign loans to the exhibition.

James Elliott
Director
University Art Museum, Berkeley

7

Self-portrait, 1910 (cat. 83)

Juan Gris: The "Perfect" Cubist

by Mark Rosenthal

Gertrude Stein called Juan Gris "a perfect painter,"[1] and it is not difficult
to appreciate her characterization. In a painting by him we find an intensely
satisfying, hermetic relationship of pictorial elements, one balanced by the
next and then another, until the subtlety of resonance reaches an exquisite
pitch. The pictures demonstrate an equally refined relationship between
the abstract play of forms and their starting point in the natural world. This
dialectic unites, too, the theoretically pure image of an object and the
existence of it as witnessed by an individual in time and space. Thus, if
perfection represents, among other things, wholeness, purity, and the
achievement of an absolute, then Gris's finest works are worthy of the
appellation "perfect."

To attain so acutely rich an art, Gris became a Cubist. More than a style,
it was, by his own description, a state of mind for him. In it was contained
"every manifestation of contemporary thought."[2] Only with Cubism,
then, did Gris have the pictorial and theoretical wherewithal to represent the
world in a thoroughly contemporary manner. But a principal goal for him
was the reconciliation of this modern expression with the great painting
traditions of history.

Amédée Ozenfant called Gris "a specialist in museums."[3] Gris wrote,
"I cannot break away from the Louvre. Mine is the method of all times, the
method used by the old masters."[4] A student of most periods of art, he
was especially drawn to the Baroque and the French eighteenth-century
schools, and in particular to Chardin. Within the old master tradition of still
life, explicitly allegorical and symbolic subjects often occur. Gris must
have found riveting the potential for secular subjects to have metaphysical
meaning, because, though he hated conventional religion, he valued
what he termed "spiritual" qualities in art.[5] Spanish still life, which Gris
would have known well from his youth in Madrid, epitomized the atmosphere of transubstantiation. The object is treated with enormous reverence
and emotion and is, in effect, elevated to a religious level.[6] Stein wrote
that for Gris "still life was not a seduction it was a religion."[7] He had a deep
regard for such lessons of history, saying that "quality" in an artist was

shown by the quantity of the past in his work.[8]

Gris reflected his knowledge and integration of old master still life in fundamental ways. Many works show his consciousness of traditional iconographic patterns. Most telling, however, is his reverence for the object, especially in contrast to his colleagues in Cubism, Pablo Picasso and Georges Braque. Like the masters of still life, Gris developed his own repertoire of objects. He always emphasized that his pictures showed the emotion he had with regard to the objects therein,[9] and that great art requires a careful choice of subject.[10] So devoted was he to the object and its inherent power of suggestion that whenever he verged on non-objectivity, he would turn away. Hence, he could speak of his work as possessing not only pictorial structure but poetic metaphor.[11]

Symbols were anathema for Gris. Rather, he composed and thought in metaphorical terms. Maurice Raynal, with whom he generally agreed on aesthetic issues,[12] wrote that pictorial/poetic metaphor was a necessity for Gris.[13] Like Mallarmé, Gris expected to evoke certain sensations and meaningful suggestions simply by virtue of the lyric effect with which he described an object in combination with other objects. Thus, just as Gris's evolution should be described in stylistic terms, it should also be seen as a gradual formation of a personal vocabulary and iconography. In this development will emerge a characterization of Gris as a metaphysician.

Fig. 1   Illustration from "Bruits de geurre et bruits de paix," *L'Assiette au Beurre*, October 3, 1908, p. 439. Courtesy of the Main Library, University of California, Berkeley

—There was a time, young man, when I was a pacificist. But with age I've realized that our country's honor must be defended.
—With my blood?
—Well not with mine, by Jove.

Beginnings: 1887–1912

It has been claimed that Gris had "no real history" before joining Picasso and Braque.[14] Although the comment is founded on the absence of much artistic production, it is, nonetheless, too hasty in dismissing some clearly formative experiences. Born in Madrid in 1887, José Victoriano Carmelo Carlos González Pérez, later known as Juan Gris, studied engineering at the School of Arts and Industries. But he quickly developed an enthusiasm for painting, whereupon he entered the studio of an official painter named José Moreno Carbonero in 1904. The experience was negative: Carbonero "gave me a distaste for *good* painting."[15] Although apparently without merit, this training did provide the eventual benefit of pushing Gris away from "good painting" and toward the avant-garde and Art Nouveau.

The year 1906 was full of developments and proved a turning point for the young Spaniard. He began to publish satirical drawings in a Madrid magazine much imbued with the Art Nouveau spirit of mordant social criticism. An admirer of similar German periodicals, *Simplicissimus* and

Fig. 2 Illustration from "Le tabac," *L'Assiette au Beurre*, May 29, 1909, p. 984.
Courtesy of the Main Library, University of California, Berkeley

—The little baroness lights that gentleman up, wouldn't you say?
—It's wasted effort, my good fellow, he's a tobacco engineer . . . he won't catch fire!

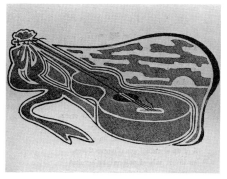

Fig. 3 Illustration from *Alma América, Poemas indo-españoles*, by José Santos Chocano, 1906, p. 237.
The Museum of Modern Art, New York
The Louis E. Stern Collection

Jugend,[16] the impressionable young man reflected the influence of that type of humor as well as the style of Art Nouveau known as *Jugendstil* (figs. 1 and 2). During the spring of 1906, he illustrated a volume of poetry entitled *Alma América* by a Peruvian named José Santos Chocano. This commission gave Gris an opportunity to exercise his more poetic nature, and it was a startling prediction of future work (fig. 3). Gris himself must have recognized some kind of breakthrough, because in this book appears for perhaps the first time his now familiar pseudonym.[17]

There is only conjecture about how or why Gris chose his pseudonym. The most frequent suggestion is that he wanted to make some gesture of independence from his background.[18] Also, giving himself a name that is a color bestows an attribute identifying him as an artist. The fact that *gris* is both Spanish and French for "gray"[19] makes him an artist in two countries and indicates not so much a streak of independence as a past identity carried into a future life. Gris's wordplay reveals an inventiveness that was consistent throughout his career and must have derived in part from his love of poetry.

In September, Gris made a more overt break with his background. He became, in effect, a "fugitive" from Spain by departing for Paris without having first served in the military. This status would hurt him, for he never was able to obtain a passport to travel.[20]

On arriving in France, Gris had but sixteen francs with which to start his residence as an artist. Luck was with him, however; a painter friend from Madrid named Daniel Vásquez Díaz immediately introduced him to another countryman, Pablo Picasso. Gris was able to move into the building in which Picasso lived, Le Bateau Lavoir at 13, rue Ravignan, and from then on was witness to the birth and evolution of Cubism. Gris writes that he "fell straight into the studio of Picasso, where I quickly met the gang of Apollinaire, Salmon, Max [Jacob], etc."[21] The spirit of the Bateau Lavoir would have confirmed much that was just emerging in the young man's outlook. Poets and artists joined forces, sharing similar aspirations and concerns. A new aesthetic was at hand, with sources as diverse as Mallarmé's poetry and African tribal art. The humor of the satirical magazines was obvious and pedestrian compared to the inspired parody and wit of the Bateau Lavoir habitués. Jokes understood only by the participants were invented. The studio of Picasso was indeed an atelier training ground for Gris, and Picasso, six years older, was a teacher-mentor-example to the new arrival. Others with whom he became acquainted early on included Braque, co-founder of Cubism, and Daniel-Henry Kahnweiler, dealer of Picasso and Braque. Kahnweiler became Gris's closest friend and most important biographer.[22]

Gris's passion for work is well known,[23] yet the character of his output until 1911 is meagerly documented. To support himself, he continued doing satirical drawings for both French and Spanish publications. Though ostensibly without direct influence on his earliest known painting, these nonetheless provided signals of later work. Art Nouveau stylizations dictated powerful juxtapositions of shapes, foreground-background reversals, patterning, and visual rhyming, all of which became characteristic of his mature work. More personal traits are present as well, such as the predilection for prominent wall patterns, mirrors, doors, and windows (figs. 1 and 2).

Besides these drawings and a few still-life studies on paper, only one painting is extant from the early years. Owned by his son, the picture is dated 1910. It seems inconceivable that these were Gris's only efforts while in the meantime Picasso and Braque were in the immediate vicinity producing Cubist paintings. The suggestion that he was at least thinking deeply about the latest problems in art comes from an anecdote by the Futurist Gino Severini in which he reports that by 1910 the poet Pierre Reverdy had become friends with Gris and visited him "to exercise his critical spirit."[24] Gris's thinking must have sharpened not only by watching his colleagues but also through his own tentative efforts. One must conclude that Gris destroyed a large body of work preceding 1911, just as in subsequent years he often threw out pictures that did not satisfy him and requested that Kahnweiler and his wife destroy all preparatory drawings.

Siphon and Bottles, 1910 (cat. 1), is notable for reasons other than its survival. Though reflecting the influence of Cézanne, the painting illustrates a synthesizing spirit that will typify Gris's entire output. On one hand, the picture has the somber mood and shallow perspective space of a Spanish Baroque still life, qualities that will occur often in Gris's work. But on the other hand, no earlier Spaniard, or even Cézanne, ever painted a siphon. Its presence in the painting bestows a certain modernity of spirit in an otherwise traditional portrayal, an awareness of the emblems of modern life found also in Gris's caricatures (fig. 4).

Gris sweepingly embraced the modern style of Cubism in 1911. Within the year, he explored the new language of Paris from its beginnings to the conceptual level reached by Picasso and Braque at that time. Initially, the problem for him was one of abstracting, that is, fracturing aspects of an object into facets. But in *The Book* (cat. 2), and other works of early 1911, the foreground-background distinction is still intact. (The book, like the siphon, is a recurring object in Gris's still lifes.) The facets are further abstracted in *Houses in Paris*, 1911 (cat. 4). For instance, the edges of the side of the building delineate a now mostly flattened, geometrical shape. Shadows are made rectilinear and are confined to arbitrary planes. In this work Gris makes a contemporary outdoor setting the subject for a modern stylization, much as was being done by Robert Delaunay and

Fig. 4 Illustration from "Les veuves," *L'Assiette au Beurre*, November 13, 1909, p. 1366.
Courtesy of the Main Library,
University of California, Berkeley

—Well, well! So you're a widow! I didn't even know you were married.
—No I wasn't; but the uniform is so becoming to blonds, especially those who are going to request a favor or some service.

Siphon and Bottles, 1910 (cat. 1)

Self-portrait, 1910–11 (cat. 84)

Cup and Glass, 1911 (cat. 85)

15

The Book, 1911 (cat. 2)

Bottle and Pitcher, 1911 (cat. 3)

Flowers in a Vase, 1911–12 (cat. 87)

Fernand Léger in their studies of urban Paris.

In *Houses in Paris—Place Ravignan*, 1911 (cat. 5), Gris disrupts the pattern of geometricized forms with the suggested structure of diagonal shafts of light emanating from a single source at the upper left. These light rays segment the ostensibily flattened, geometrical areas and, along with the modulated shadows, suggest three-dimensionality. Indeed, there is a sense of fluctuation from two- to three-dimensionality and vice versa throughout. Also striking is the vibrant rhythm of curved lines that seem to denote trees and clouds, or perhaps clouds of smoke as in contemporary work by Léger.[25] These forms have an ebullient, abstract quality, contrasting strongly with the more rectilinear, representational shapes of the houses.

Houses in Paris—Place Ravignan is still transitional in that Gris has not yet fully made background space assume tangible form. But in the more or less simultaneous portraits *Maurice Raynal* and *Señor Legua*, 1911,[26] and in *Bottle and Pitcher*, 1911 (cat. 3), he takes another step. Contours begin to break or become continuous with force lines defining the background. Then, in *Head of a Woman*, 1911–12 (cat. 86), and *Self-portrait*, 1912 (cat. 88), facial details are compartmentalized in an abstract structure as Gris further breaks up a subject according to a system of interlocking planes of shadow and light. These planes form a relief-map surface and offer great liberties of portrayal. In the former drawing a double visage appears, perhaps for the first time in the twentieth century.

While Gris is reaching a stage of development comparable to that of Picasso and Braque, he is nonetheless creating works that *look* quite different. Most noticeable is the rigorous structure; it is as if a straight-edge had been in use, and every shadow had been planned if not observed. Perhaps because Gris was so interested in an undulating surface, he continued to employ a modicum of color—mostly blues, greens, and grays —whereas his colleagues were limiting their palettes. While Picasso and Braque sought integration of figure and ground by eliminating shadow, systematically linking object contours with structural ones, and creating planar, cipherlike units, Gris maintained a rich, tactile surface through the use of light and shade. His decision to include shadow stemmed from a desire to relate his form of Cubism with the conventions of traditional still-life painting. Clearly, the longstanding problem of the play of light on an object remained at the center of his concerns.

During 1912 Gris continued to investigate the systematic integration of representational detail and structure. In *Still Life with Oil Lamp* (cat. 8), light rays create a united surface; yet the boundaries of each ray are not maintained from the upper left corner to the lower right. Rather, contours of the lamps intermingle or join the rays. A gem among the entire 1912 series, this work is notable for its utterly luminous grays and whites on

Houses in Paris, 1911 (cat. 4)

Houses in Paris—Place Ravignan, 1911 (cat. 5)

Head of a Woman, 1911 (cat. 86)

Self-portrait, 1912 (cat. 88)

a field of blue and green tones. About Gris's color of 1912, Apollinaire compares its "effect to the bluish flame of gas stoves."[27]

Portrait of the Artist's Mother, 1912 (cat. 7), is based on a disjointed structure complemented by a fractured visage. There is the suggestion that a diagonal and a horizontal-vertical cross underlie the composition. Within the now skewed arrangement of sections are merged the details of the full face and profile. Yet the head seems barely to sustain its position against the seeming rotation of the pictorial structure. Gris is fond of showing this process by which he dynamically manipulates a subject; he even rhapsodizes on the curvature of the lower jaw, rhythmically repeating its now geometric form. There is a comic note in these deliberate, satirical manipulations that also rings constantly in the work of Gris's colleagues at the Bateau Lavoir.

A more serious tone is struck by Gris's *Portrait of Picasso* (cat. 6). With its exhibition at the Salon des Indépendants early in 1912, Gris suddenly took a position among the Cubists. And because Picasso and Braque had not shown in years, the portrait made Gris the link to the founders of the movement.[28] At the lower right corner Gris indicates his admiration for the older Spanish painter with the inscription *Hommage à Pablo Picasso, Juan Gris*. Perhaps in creating the picture, Gris consciously made reference to Picasso's own *portrait-hommage* to Gertrude Stein, 1906 (fig. 5). Although leaning in opposite directions, both subjects have similar hand positions, disjointed eyes, and poses cut off at the knees; and each figure possesses a hulking solidity. One difference in the portrayals is Gris's consciousness of a certain tradition of portraiture. Revealing his close attention to the old masters, he includes an attribute—a palette—to better identify the sitter as a painter. Once more the light emanating from a single source, taking the form of vectors throughout the background,[29] helps unite the diverse parts and adds to the pearly quality of the blues. One of Picasso's and Braque's concerns was to give tangible form to empty space, and often this notation was accomplished in summary fashion. Gris's solution is for background space to be embodied as light which assumes distinct form. Even though Gris refuses to interrupt many of the contours forming the body, unity of surface and space is nevertheless achieved, because the light washing the whole produces a fluid pattern of shapes. Each shape has an abstract life within the rippling, relief-surface structure. Figure and ground lie on one layer that is essentially without plunges in depth.

A second major exhibition occurred in 1912 in Paris, and again Gris was a notable figure. Held at Galerie la Boétie from October 10, the exhibition *La section d'or* included Jacques Villon, Raymond Duchamp-Villon, Marcel Duchamp, Albert Gleizes, Jean Metzinger, Francis Picabia, Fernand Léger, Roger de La Fresnaye, André Lhote, Marie Laurencin,

Fig. 5 Pablo Picasso
Gertrude Stein, 1906
Oil on canvas
100 x 81.3 cm (39⅜ x 32 in.)
The Metropolitan Museum of Art
Bequest of Gertrude Stein, 1946

Portrait of Picasso, 1912 (cat. 6)

Portrait of the Artist's Mother, 1912 (cat. 7)

Still Life with Oil Lamp, 1912 (cat. 8)

Banjo and Glasses, 1912 (cat. 9)

Louis Marcoussis, and Alexander Archipenko. Absent as usual were Picasso and Braque, but the exhibition, nevertheless, significantly enhanced the position of Cubism. From the group, Gris was singled out by Maurice Raynal as "the fiercest of the purists."[30] His application of a mirror to a canvas[31] instead of applying paint to imitate the object was startling and caused early notice of the collage technique invented a few months earlier by Picasso and Braque.

The *Section d'or* exhibition developed from discussions held at the home of Villon in the suburb of Puteaux beginning in 1911. The group devoted great attention to mathematical and scientific questions. Evoking these concerns, Guillaume Apollinaire in a speech at the opening of an exhibition in 1911 said, "Geometry is to the plastic arts what grammar is to the art of the writer."[32] In this spirit the Puteaux group named itself the Golden Section, as if to alter the emphasis from the name Cubism which had been given with great derision. Now an abstract, pure idea of proportion was emphasized. The group developed a theory that a continuous tradition of proportion existed in French painting; they sought to join that line of evolution. Gris's interest in these problems continued well past this period, but he would always emphasize that a proportional system was only the basis of a composition, not an end in itself.[33]

It is likely that Gris was already considering various formulas in 1911. The aforementioned *Houses in Paris—Place Ravignan* of that year was chosen for inclusion in the *Section d'or* exhibition and is dedicated to a Puteaux colleague, Picabia. It exhibits a formula that would occur frequently in 1912. The abrupt horizontal delineating the roof line on the façade of the central building divides the height of the picture at about three-quarters. The golden section is closer to about three-fifths. Gris would use both these proportions often in 1912.[34]

Another work shown in the *Section d'or* exhibition was *Man in the Café*, 1912 (cat. 10), which reflects the humorous mode of Gris's earlier caricatures. Now the top-hatted gentleman, who was usually an object of scorn in the satirical magazines, finds himself in a Cubist stronghold. Gris makes that clear for insiders by the lettering *PIC* and *AP*, which must refer to Picasso and Apollinaire. Later, Kasimir Malevich in *An Englishman in Moscow*, 1914 (fig. 6), would likewise show a visiting gentleman in an alien environment.[35] The Russian could have known Gris's picture in reproduction, as it was illustrated in Apollinaire's *Les peintres cubistes*, published in Paris in 1913.

The vertical dimension of *Man in the Café* is divided with a decisive horizontal line through the head of the figure, again at about three-quarters the height of the painting. The horizontal dimension is cut by a vertical line left of center. The proportions of the parts to one another and these to the overall dimensions are close to the formula of the golden section.

Fig. 6   Kasimir Malevich
An Englishman in Moscow, 1914
Oil on canvas
86.4 x 56.5 cm. (34 x 22¼ in.)
Stedelijk Museum, Amsterdam

Study for "Man in the Café," 1912 (cat. 90)

Man in the Café, 1912 (cat. 10)

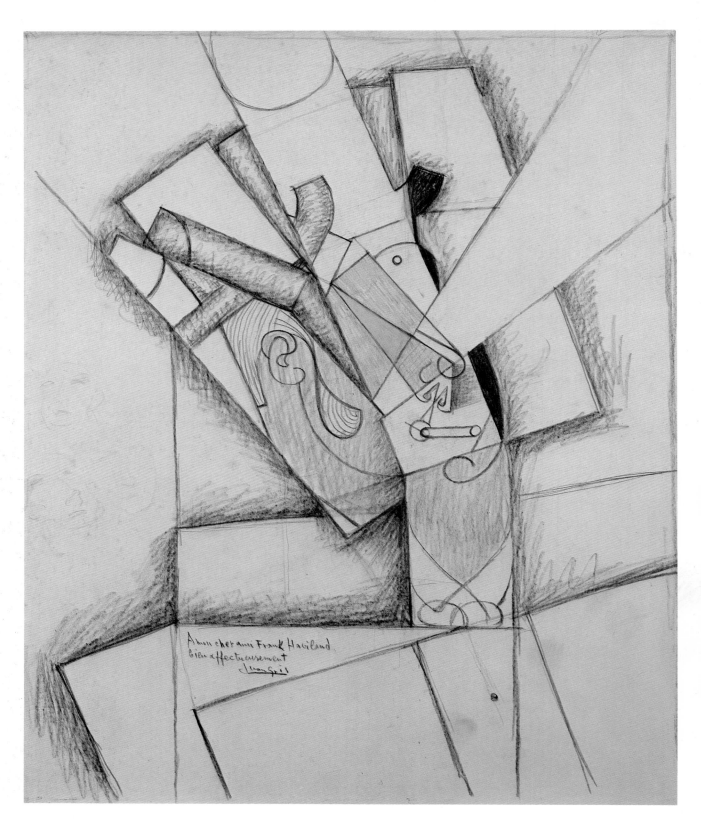

Study for "The Smoker," 1912 (cat. 89)

The Smoker, 1913 (fig. 7)

Fig. 7 (See p. 33)
The Smoker, 1913
Oil on canvas
73 x 54 cm. (28¾ x 21¼ in.)
Thyssen-Bornemisza Collection,
Lugano, Switzerland

Fig. 8 Paul Cézanne
Black Clock, 1869–71
Oil on canvas
55.2 x 74.3 cm. (21¾ x 29¼ in.)
Stavros S. Niarchos Collection

However, Gris never precisely duplicated the formula in his calculations for the composition of a picture, perhaps leaving a final decision to intuition or aesthetic calculation.

The division of *Man in the Café* renders a thematic separation, as well. The left portion of the picture is the world of appearances, for the buildings and the hand and foot of the figure are shown more or less representationally. On the right side is the realm of art: the second foot is tipped up so as to become a flat plane, the other hand loses some of its three-dimensionality, and the head is undergoing metamorphosis.

Comparison of the drawn study for *Man in the Café* (cat. 90) and the painting, as well as the charcoal *Smoker*, 1912 (cat. 89), with the later 1913 painting (fig. 7) is revealing. Gris's extant drawings are virtually plans for paintings. Indeed, they have a completeness, demonstrating Gris's rigor and care, that belies the preparatory character they have in the artistic process.

The contrast between an anecdotal world of appearance and a realm of metamorphosis, as in *Man in the Café*, is a hallmark of Gris's art starting with the works he showed at the *Section d'or* exhibition. In *The Watch*, 1912 (cat. 11), the contrast manifests itself in the realism of execution used for the curtain and the reconstituted, synthetic reality elsewhere. It is as if the curtain is pulled back for our entrance from the perceptual world to another, Cubist milieu. Such an allegorical juxtaposition is not present in the work of Braque and Picasso, although they had been concerned with providing "real details" as clues to the identity of the subject transformed.[36] Gris wants, instead, either to compare easily comprehended identities and their renderings or, on occasion, to wittily subvert the relationship. For instance, he writes GUITARRA on what is a banjo in *Banjo and Glasses*, 1912 (cat. 9). That there are such important differences between Gris and the founders of Cubism merely one and a half years after the former had joined the movement shows the extent of his independent character. Indeed, many other aspects of *The Watch* indicate Gris's already unique style: the black linear "grillwork" through which the objects are seen, the sensuousness of color, the considerable number of views synthesized in one image, the use of the wallpaper pattern to activate the background space and make solid the void, and the great fluctuation between two- and three-dimensionality without seeming to sacrifice the surface to depth.

It is instructive to compare *The Watch* with Cézanne's *Black Clock*, 1869–71 (fig. 8).[37] In both, the depiction of a fabric and timepiece is central to the composition. But there is an obvious evolution in style and proportional systems. Cézanne's canvas is divided symmetrically by the horizontal line of the table surface and the vertical right edge of the wall molding; the former dimension is also divided precisely in thirds. Gris, too,

The Watch, 1912 (cat. 11)

The Siphon, 1913 (cat. 14)

emphasizes a sense of geometric proportions, but his are based on the golden section. The prominent horizontal occurs at approximately three-fifths the height. A quasi two-three-two rhythm is used to divide the horizontal. Apart from these differences, Gris often followed Cézanne's example, especially his regard for the still-life subject.

So interested was Gris in these mathematical ratios for developing pictures that he, at this time, chose to number his works rather than give titles. Raynal said that this practice showed "the study of forms is his only concern."[38] It is important to remark again, however, that Gris did not follow the golden section proportions precisely, nor did he repeat a formula.

Gris adopted the practice of Picasso and Braque at this time by signing an exclusive contract with Kahnweiler at the conclusion of the *Section d'or* exhibition, whereupon, like his colleagues, he no longer participated in salon exhibitions.

An Independent Voice: 1913 to 1914

Fresh from his exhibition successes, and strengthened by his contract with Kahnweiler and the beginning of his relationship with Josette Herpin, who would become his lifelong companion, Gris started work in 1913 with a spirit of enthusiasm and independence. As Cubism developed into the Pan-European language of the avant-garde, Gris moved to the forefront in artistic creativity and influence.[39] Most immediately notable about his work was the variety and strength of his color. Unmatched by Picasso and Braque in this regard, Gris employed color in a rich and complex manner. With this added element, his pictures took on an intensely refined subtlety that would characterize his work for the remainder of this career.

The Siphon (cat. 14), *Guitar on Table* (cat. 13), and *Glass of Beer and Playing Cards*, (cat. 12), all 1913, are good examples of his new-found strength. In each, bits of detail identify objects and render them tangibly present in the picture; yet juxtaposed are abstract areas that seem to represent nothing. Both situations may become reversed, as when the detail of an object assumes a non-objective, purely pictorial function, and an "abstract" shape becomes discernible, for example, as a section of light. Especially paradoxical are the areas painted in *trompe l'oeil* fashion to imitate a marbleized table top, wallpaper, or wood paneling, as if part of a collage. Seemingly abstract and representational at the same time, these areas rhyme with one another texturally. The pictures are at once the recording of a still-life scene and the transformation of such a situation into an exercise in pictorial pyrotechnics.

Guitar on Table, 1913 (cat. 13)

Glass of Beer and Playing Cards, 1913 (cat. 12)

The siphon is enclosed within the stripe that forms part of the composition of the work. The origin of these stripes is unclear, but they were predicted in Picasso's and Braque's *papiers collés*, Gris's own light bands of 1911–12, and his grillwork and wallpaper patterns of late 1912. He made details subservient to the stripes, yet was playfully reluctant to completely flatten all elements. Hence the siphon nozzle, and the pipe bowl in *Glass of Beer*, have considerable importance, interrupting the flat surface in their aggressive, three-dimensional push out from the canvas.

Jean Cocteau reported Gris saying, "It was I . . . who introduced the siphon bottle into painting"; the writer further indicates that the statement was not facetious.[40] Gris's pride had to do with the importance of specific objects to him, and the use of these by members of his milieu. A decade later, Léger, too, would make prominent use of the siphon as a totem of modern life and mechanized society.[41] Gris's intentions were, no doubt, similar. However, for him, unlike Léger, the object reinforced the modernity of a Cubist statement, especially in comparison to earlier still-life traditions.

The pipe, like the siphon, is probably not gratuitously chosen. Mallarmé had used it extensively in his poetry, and the object has a history in Gris's caricatures as part of a sexual joke (figs. 9 and 10). Not only is it a phallic symbol, but the pipe replaces or supercedes sex in the satirical drawings. Such hidden associations and jokes were characteristic of the milieu. André Salmon wrote of the Bateau Lavoir group, "We invented an artificial world with countless jokes, rites and expressions that were quite unintelligible to others."[42] In that spirit, perhaps the siphon also should be understood as a sexual symbol.

A tour de force in this series of works involving a structure of stripes is the brilliantly colored *Landscape with Houses at Céret*, 1913 (cat. 18). During the summer of 1913, Gris joined Picasso at Céret, where he painted this rare pure landscape. In it, he loosened the vertical emphasis of the earlier stripes so as to form a composition of diagonal, overlapping planes. Once more, the structure appears to be the starting point of the painting, and all details conform to it.

Contemporary with these virtuoso performances of controlling his subject are pictures with more monumental themes than that represented by the siphon. Among the earliest examples of this rather un-Cubist approach is *The Guitar*, 1913 (cat. 16), a major work according to one of his letters,[43] which exhibits a kind of allegorical juxtaposition. The photograph of a Corot- or Goya-like mother and child suggests an exterior, three-dimensional world, untouched and sentimental, whereas the marbleized area at the lower right matter-of-factly asserts the surface plane of the picture. At center is the rendering of a guitar which has a certain metamorphic quality.

Landscape with Houses at Céret, 1913 (cat. 18)

The Guitar, 1913 (cat. 16)

The Bottle of Claret, 1913 (cat. 17)

Untitled (Violin and Ink Bottle on a Table), 1913 (cat. 15)

Gris wrote that "the essence of painting is the expression of certain relationships between the painter and the outside world. . . ."[44] His friend Raynal described how Gris started a painting: "The emotion felt by Juan Gris before some object suggests to him the invention of his project."[45] Picasso in his earlier career had acted on such emotions, too. Fernand Olivier wrote that the guitar recalled powerful memories of Spain for him;[46] one can surmise the same of Gris, who would break down in tears when he heard Spanish music.[47] In the Picasso-edited periodical, *Arte Joven*, published in Madrid at the turn of the century, an article appeared on the "Psychology of the Guitar." In it, the instrument is a "symbol of the popular soul." Such implications were not alien to Gris, for in the 1906 *Alma América* series, a drawing of a guitar before the sea illustrates the poem titled *The Minstrel's Soul* (fig. 3). If the guitar evokes the soul of the minstrel or, more generally, the artist, the area at the lower right of *The Guitar* shows the artifice of the artist, and the mother and child indicate the anecdotal world from which he transposes his creations. By contrast with the sensuously described sections in the corners, the guitar has a lucid, dignified presence similar to that of Gris himself. As opposed to the siphon, which epitomizes popular café life, the guitar provides a deeply personal evocation. It becomes a leitmotif in Gris's art from this time forward.

A second instance of this more serious approach to subject matter is the stately *Violin and Ink Bottle on a Table* (cat. 15), painted a month earlier, in April 1913. Here, another musical instrument assumes the central position on the canvas. Conceptually, it and the ink bottle are the tools of an artist. This thematic parallel is reinforced by a formal rhyme; both implements have hollow interiors and fluted exteriors. Painted to resemble a collage, the picture reveals a broad interplay of plastic interests. Especially notable are the visual tensions between airy, spacious sections and constricted, airless, energetic ones. Plunges in depth are brought up short by surface-stressing, contiguous planes. The violin strings seem to jut forward from the picture plane, yet are held in check by the surface-hugging rectangle in which they are contained. Gris's handling of black in this painting would be repeated frequently in subsequent work. Here the blacks serve as shadows, reversals of nearby forms, three-dimensional edges, and abstract shapes.

The Guitar and *Violin and Ink Bottle* embody a form of Cubism that is distinct from that of its inventors. Gris's approach to the object included an analytical depiction and a characterization of it, along with an interest in his own perception of and emotion before it. Picasso was generally playful or manipulative and in control of his motif. Whereas Picasso seemed to create a painting by a process of accretion, that is, adding one texture or facet to another, Gris started with a complete structural armature and added yet more complexity. He was a master of compositional drama, integrating his interest and analysis of an object with a forceful presentation. He quite obviously sought timelessness, and his majestic objects fit into a tradition of still life.

Picasso and Braque were not unmindful of traditional still-life conventions to which their own work might relate. Braque employed the guitar in an allegorical manner, symbolizing both music and art,[48] from as early as 1908. And Braque's influence on Gris was enormous; he wrote, "I was such an admirer of his painting that I was being crushed by it."[49] Ultimately, Gris utilized the allegorical approach more fully than his colleagues and looked to the traditions themselves for inspiration.

Gris was especially mindful of the traditions of French Classicism and Spanish Baroque still life. Like the French, Gris always strove for rich textural compositions rendered in narrow spaces. French allegories of knowledge, art, and the senses would have been important to him, too. To the Spanish he owed his emphasis on the object, that is, its shape and how light falls on it; the use of geometry to elevate lowly subjects; the considerable solemnity of portrayal; and, from Spanish Realism, the powerful foreground lighting and brooding shadows and blacks.

Violin and Guitar (cat. 19) is another of these magisterial statements that marked 1913 as the beginning of Gris's mature art. Here he combines the inherent dignity and poetic quality of the objects with an exploration of their three-dimensional aspects. An essentially cruciform composition underlies the whole and lends a hierarchical air; however, as with his use of the golden section, Gris was never absolutely precise in making his measurements fit a predetermined scheme. The painting is built on a series of pictorial rhymes among the forms of the guitar, violin, and glass. Gris's predilection for rhymes, or rhythms based on visual similarities, has been compared to the techniques of the poets who were so much a part of his milieu,[50] but it can also be found in the art of his colleagues. More fundamentally poetic is the spirited flight of artistic manipulation that occurs in the central section, juxtaposed with the conventional world symbolized by the wood molding, wallpaper, and floorboards of a surrounding room. These background details establish a representational setting as well as a pictorial plane of possibilities. This richly detailed room should be seen as having fantastic associations for Gris since he reportedly lived in utter squalor.

As we have seen, Gris had imitated the *trompe l'oeil* play of *papier collé* by painting illusionistic textures early in 1913. Toward the end of the year, he found it harder and harder to resist the alluring potential of this technique. With it, a surface could be completely covered and activated in all sections, a possibility in which Gris had always shown an interest. In *Violin and Checkerboard* (cat. 20) and *Pears and Grapes on a Table*

Violin and Guitar, 1913 (cat. 19)

Violin and Checkerboard, 1913 (cat. 20)

Pears and Grapes on a Table, 1913 (cat. 21)

Fig. 11   (See p. 51)
Glasses, Teacup, Bottle, and Pipe on a Table, 1914
Oil, *papier collé* and fusain on canvas
65 x 92 cm. (25⅝ x 36¼ in.)
Kunstsammlung Nordrhein-Westfalen, Düsseldorf
(DC 87)

Fig. 12   (See p. 52)
Breakfast, 1914
Papier collé, crayon, and oil on canvas
80.9 x 59.7 cm. (31⅞ x 23½ in.)
The Museum of Modern Art, New York
Acquired through the Lillie P. Bliss Bequest
(DC 92)

(cat. 21), both 1913, he produces with paint some of the surfaces familiar from the *papier collé* of his friends. His aim, it would appear, was yet greater visual complexity than he had earlier demonstrated, for no shape in these pictures is inactive, either by virtue of color, shape, shadow, or texture. And each aspect relates to another in the composition, either rhythmically or by contrast. An underlying, cruciform structure is again perceivable in these two pictures, but Gris endlessly jostled, obviated, and reconstituted it. Indeed, we can feel his hand and intelligence at work forming and resolving contrasts.

Gris's rhyming is not only formal but thematic. The violin is shown caught in an interplay between its commonplace appearance and a manipulated state of being. Moreover, one "plays" not only the violin but the checkers and dice. The sheet music and checkerboard are conceptually alike; each is the terrain or map of a sequence of played actions. Such is Gris's wit integrated into his formal manipulations. But, also, the violin is a metaphor for artistic activity while, by contrast, the checkerboard evokes life experience.

In *Pears and Grapes on a Table*, Gris rhymed physical situations. The floor lies beneath the chair, which is, in part, beneath the table. Just as the chair holds the cloth, the dish contains the pears. He compared, too, the intellectual activity of reading the newspaper with the sensuous process of eating grapes, a combination of the Apollonian and Dionysian that is, in fact, played out on the picture plane itself.

In 1914, Gris wholeheartedly yielded to Picasso and Braque's technique of *papier collé*, where paper fragments are pasted to the picture surface (figs. 11 and 12). As usual, however, his approach was far more complex than theirs. He often covered virtually the entire canvas with an interlocking structure of diverse papers, an innovation that was intimated in the last two works discussed.[51] Each piece of paper was cut precisely to fit a place in a predetermined, abstract composition. This literal structure of parts meant that Gris had at least somewhat embraced the concept of the *tableau-objet*; that is, the importance of the artwork as a physical entity was meant to exceed its function as a medium of representation. Yet Gris was ambivalent in his allegiance to this formalist doctrine, because his decisions on the structure of the pasted papers had to do in part, also, with making each accord with a represented object. By contrast, when Picasso and Braque used a paper fragment in combination with other media, the physical independence of the paper was usually stressed, particularly by its edges being prominent. Often, no more than a few pieces of paper at most were added by Picasso and Braque; with little or no drawing on the papers, they retain their identity as "foreign" bodies attached to the surface. Gris camouflaged the edges of each paper to such an extent that it is often difficult to discern, even at close proximity, what is attached to the

Glasses, Teacup, Bottle, and Pipe on a Table, 1914 (fig. 11)

Breakfast, 1914 (fig. 12)

canvas. And when almost an entire plane is covered, the task of discernment becomes altogether futile.

A collage by Gris is an immensely subtle enterprise. Underlying is what Kahnweiler called a "flat, coloured architecture." By this he means an overall structure, largely based on regularly shaped planes that are contiguous or overlapping, such as in *Guitar, Glasses, and Bottle* (cat. 25), and *The Newspaper* (cat. 24), both 1914. Overlying is the texture of cut paper. Each fragment may have three aspects: first, as a pictorial element; second, as a sign of a representational object, by analogy of color or by containing a visual clue; third, as simply a piece of paper ("thing-in-itself"), with a certain pattern having tactile and material interest incorporated into the whole composition.[52] Adding yet further, Gris drew, painted, and/or modeled on these fragments, so that they are rarely perceived in a completely forthright manner.[53] The still-life representation, which is the outermost "skin," weaves a relationship with these structural aspects. Abstraction and representation are moot qualities in these highly refined works.

Gris greatly simplified his objects in 1914, making use especially of signs. A circle becomes the opening of a bottle, glass, guitar, teacup, or pipe. The checkerboard pattern recurs, signifying a backgammon board, tablecloth, table surface, floor, steps, or label; wood-graining may represent a table, chair, wall, or floor. Throughout, Gris maintained the integrity of his objects as, for example, he employed chiaroscuro and three-dimensionality to give prominence to them. Certain ones are ubiquitous and plastically irreducible, such as the pipe. Similarly, musical instruments and newspapers have an imperturbable character through all the collage manipulations.

The Guitar, 1914 (cat. 28), is a magnificent example of the still-present dignity of the object in Gris's work. The form of the subject is combined with an abstract structure in that the front and side views each coincide with a pictorial plane. The brown wood-graining is part of the instrument as well as the adjacent area, and the wallpaper is repeated on the edge of the guitar. The strings are placed so as to be read as part of the instrument and the abstract composition at once, thus forming an integration of subject and structure.

The violin, too, retains its wholeness and metaphoric quality in *Musician's Table*, 1914 (cat. 23). Gris utilized the standard iconography for the subject of the attributes of Music, such as was used by Chardin. That is, an instrument and sheet music are juxtaposed to convey the theme of Music. To these attributes, Gris relates others suggestive of eating and reading. A glass is drawn on the music paper, which itself is comparable to the lines of newsprint. There, the elaborate script clearly rhymes with the openings of the violin. The demonstration of artistic endeavor is

Guitar, Glasses, and Bottle, 1914 (cat. 25)

54

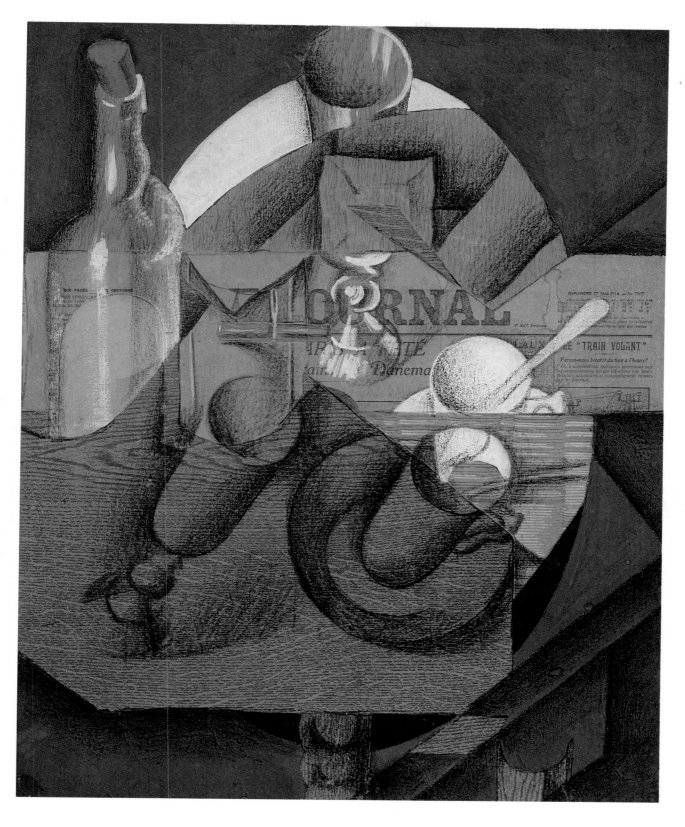

The Newspaper, 1914 (cat. 24)

The Guitar, 1914 (cat. 28)

Musician's Table, 1914 (cat. 23)

playfully brought to nought by the newspaper headlines: "Explorateurs en désaccord" and "Ils s'accusent de n'avoir rien exploré" ("Explorers clashing" and "They accuse one another of having explored nothing"). Gris seems to suggest that, after all, these Cubists are *provocateurs* who have little substance.

The hermetic and deliberately ambiguous quality of Gris's art is shown in one of the masterpieces of 1914, *The Man at the Café* (cat. 22). He recycled the "architecture" of a 1913 painting, *Guitar on a Chair* (fig. 13), in the 1914 work, in that a large rectangle atop one defined by the picture format is the structure in both. Even the rhythm of notched areas in the lower center is virtually identical. Such a repetition confirms Gris's later claim that he started with a pictorial structure and only afterward defined a subject based on it. But Gris had a catalogue of subjects to which he repeatedly returned, in this case the man in a café, as seen in 1912. Here the theme is turned into a still life of the attributes of the café dweller, such as was done in *Glass of Beer* and *The Siphon*, both 1913. The continued currency and importance of this subject for the Cubists is demonstrated by Picasso's return to it in his *Absinthe Drinker* of 1914. The newspaper headline concerning the problem of art forgeries also reflects the presence of multiple versions of the same subject as created by the Cubists.[54]

Newspapers and printed matter are a means of conveying the wit of the Cubist collagists. They call attention to their technique, and to the fact that in collage real things are added to an unreal, pictorial world.[55] Gris's wit is everywhere apparent; for example, the painted AUX on a wine bottle is the remnant of Bordeaux but alludes to *faux*, meaning false, implying that the bottle and label are illusions.[56] *Le Vrai et Le Faux* ("Truth and Falsehood") is like a credo of the collagist.[57] Another collage (fig. 11) includes a newspaper clipping showing a monument before and after defacement;[58] the photos epitomize the Cubist aesthetic of irreverent manipulation. And in *The Newspaper* (cat. 24), Gris seems to have deliberately separated the RNAL of JOURNAL in order to make reference to his friend RAYNAL.

Though Gris had managed to achieve a certain success during this phase of his career, it was as illusory and paradoxical as his artistic means. The war sent Kahnweiler packing to Switzerland, from where he sent a small stipend to the artist. But sales were meager, even though Gertrude Stein had now "discovered" Gris and done much to advance his career. Indeed, his financial situation had become desperate.

Fig. 13
Guitar on a Chair, 1913
Oil and *papier collé* on canvas
100 x 65 cm (39⅜ x 25⅝ in.)
Private collection
(DC 52)

The Man at the Café, 1914 (cat. 22)

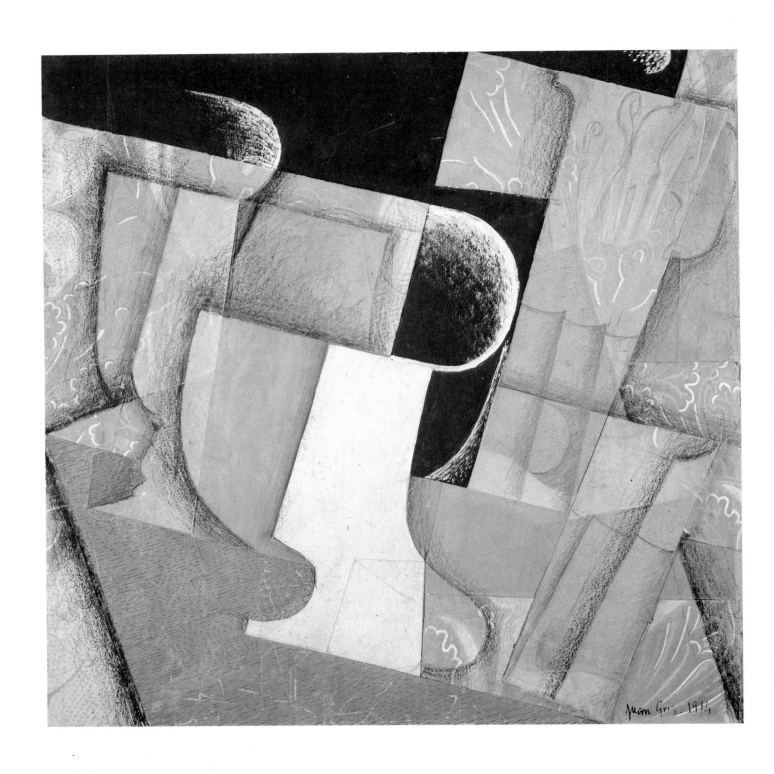

The Glass, 1914 (cat. 26)

Bottle of Banyul, 1914 (cat. 27)

Violin and Glass, 1915 (cat. 29)

Still Life with Checked Tablecloth, 1915 (cat. 30)

Book, Pipe, and Glasses, 1915 (cat. 31)

Divergent Tendencies: 1915 to 1917

After making *papier collé* exclusively for about a year, Gris stopped the activity altogether in the winter of 1914–15. Picasso ceased, too, at about the same time or shortly before, but whether the decisions were made in concert is not known. Certainly the privations of war-torn Europe must have made their reflexive collage games seem out of step with the times. The medium was not entirely in character with Gris's personal inclinations either. The momentariness of the process and the temporality of the newspaper headlines were alien to his solemn excursions toward more majestic heights. In *papier collé* flatness is overriding, whereas Gris's natural tendency was usually to juxtapose plastic passages. The medium also tended to encourage an accumulation of objects, an attribute with which Gris wanted to dispense by early 1915. In place of "inventories of objects,"[59] he sought pictorial unity.

Remarkably, Gris felt, as of March 1915, that he had no aesthetic and required further experience.[60] In this spirit, and that created by the unsettling wartime atmosphere, he alternated between stylistic poles from 1915 through 1917. In his work of this period one finds claustrophobic interiors dominated by highly charged still lifes contrasting with airy still lifes set before open windows. During these years Gris made some of his purest abstractions, as well as his most naturalistic drawings; there are culminating portrayals of favorite objects, portraits, harlequins, and even one sculpture (fig. 14). Perhaps the most jarring contrast is between the sunny, lush, pointillist paintings and the somber black ambiences that became prevalent.

Although Gris said he was finished with inventories of objects, he produced several works in early 1915 that represent a pinnacle in the complex vision initiated by the collages. One is *Book, Pipe, and Glasses* (cat. 31), which is outstanding in its dynamic interplay of diverse bodies. Still present is an inventory, including the favored subject of the book. Here it has overtones of literature and philosophy, typological parallels to the arts, contrary to its use in the earlier caricatures as the prop of a vicious judge meting out an arbitrary judgment. Gris's primary aim in the 1915 painting was pictorial, however; he wanted to unite the objects compositionally. He started by painting a large, multi-textured oval, over which he laid a parallelogram. The relationship of these to the overall format of the picture establishes the basic "architecture" of the composition. Covering the planes are objects that are generally three-dimensional; these are now rendered whole or abstracted, rather than fragmented. Each plane and object is carefully placed in space and has a clear compositional function. Volume, shading, and three-dimensionality coexist with transparency and flatness. Line and color are disassociated, too, and function either analytically, descriptively, or abstractly. The result is startling, as

Fig. 14
Harlequin, 1917
Carved and painted plaster
54 cm. high (21¼ in.)
Philadelphia Museum of Art
The A. E. Gallatin Collection

65

forms seem to be detached from, yet held in check by, the picture surface, in an effect similar to that of the multiple veils or skins of 1914. As complex as the work is, there is an elementary boldness and wholeness about it.

The rediscovery of volume is accompanied by a greater sense of abstraction generally. *Violin and Glass*, 1915 (cat. 29), recalls such works of 1913 as *Violin and Checkerboard* (cat. 20) in its combination of three-dimensionality and flat patterning. But here the identity of the instrument is greatly abbreviated. Thus stimulated, in June of 1915 Gris painted *Still Life* (cat. 32), a work with seemingly no subject at all. Founded in an overlapping pattern of flat planes is an intricate arrangement of two- and three-dimensional forms. The generally hermetic quality of Gris's art, with each detail rhythmically repeated, reversed, or balanced, lent itself to this foray into abstraction. He followed it with works such as *The Cherries* (cat. 34), in which the hard, solid forms are replaced by a combination of textural surfaces. Compared to *Still Life*, Gris retreated somewhat by including slight references to recognizable objects.[61]

When *Still Life* was made, Gris wrote, "My painting is much less dry and more plastic."[62] Since the well-known *Still Life before an Open Window: Place Ravignan* (cat. 33), also dated June, is representational at heart, Gris's statement suggests that he was more interested in plasticity than whether or not the picture was non-objective. In this breakthrough work, Gris attempted to bring indoor and outdoor views to the same plane. A still life fills the foreground and is juxtaposed with a simply rendered street scene. Along the sides of the picture, the window frame and railing create transitions between the interior and exterior. The scale relationships of the key elements—the bottle of Médoc, the window frame and trees—are such as to suggest Gris might have actually determined the proper sizes as if in perspective before enforcing the rule of the plane.

While the distinction between the representational world and the artistically manipulated still life recalls the juxtaposition in *Man in the Café*, 1912, Gris at this point added content to the exterior locale. That is, the square has a dreamy, blue-tinged, otherworldly quality reminiscent of exterior views found in Renaissance and Baroque paintings of open windows. Matisse's treatment of the luxuriant world seen through a window would have become known to Gris when the two became close friends during the preceding fall at Collioure. But even if Matisse influenced Gris's turn to the open window theme,[63] the latter would have been acquainted with many other versions of the subject—from Renaissance and Baroque depictions to those of the nineteenth century—in his museum haunts. In general, the window is an opening to the natural world which is distinctly transcendent when compared to an interior space.[64] During the nineteenth century, the subject referred specifically to a dilemma of artists and poets that would not have been unknown to Gris himself. The

Still Life, 1915 (cat. 32)

The Cherries, 1915 (cat. 34)

Still Life before an Open Window: Place Ravignan, 1915 (cat. 33)

nineteenth-century artist was torn between the worlds of nature and art. Though longing for the immensity beyond, by remaining in his studio the artist retained the "poetry of possession."[65] Gris gave the theme a personal cast by unveiling the scene outside his own window. His dilemma, then, was between a sensuous, almost Symbolist world and a realm of the intellect, where he could control his physical motifs.

Gris followed *Place Ravignan* with several other works which had more radiant, outdoor settings, as if he had given in to the attractions of nature that summer. Notable is *The Pot of Geraniums*, 1915 (cat. 35), in which the still life seems almost to have left the interior for an existence in a landscape. The pattern of leaves and rhythm of blues subsume the implicit room in the sunlit, surrounding space. Only the edges of a window frame, table, and railing indicate an interior, as Gris foregoes the drama of the open window metaphor in favor of a purely sensuous rendering. Not inappropriately, Douglas Cooper has proposed the influence of Matisse in this brilliantly colored work.[66]

Within a month of the completion of *The Pot of Geraniums*, Gris began a group of somber paintings. In *Fantômas* (cat. 36) and *The Bottle of Claret* (fig. 15) of 1915, there is a palpable gloom created by the ambience of blacks and browns. Within dark interiors, Gris describes extremely shallow spaces of one plane laid over or adjacent to another. White lines, seemingly the last notes added,[67] schematically provide three-dimensional definition. In the title, he alludes to a fictional criminal named Fantômas who was known for his sleight of hand,[68] thereby likening his Cubist tricks to those of a legendary predecessor.

In subsequent months Gris continued to explore these shallow spaces but reintroduced brilliant color into his work. *Guitar on a Table*, 1915 (cat. 38), exhibits in the confined space created by overlapping color planes a conception very similar to that in *Fantômas*. The white lines again define an object resting atop the layers. Whereas the yellows in the latter work have a precious, discrete presence, the blue in the former seems to expand and permeate the picture. The blues in *Guitar on a Table* and *Place Ravignan* should be compared, for they form a rhymed, poetic likeness of pure realms of experience. Whereas Gris had in *Musician's Table*, 1914, suggested the concept of music by the representation of its attributes, in *Guitar* he makes the subject immanent, assuming an epic simplicity. Kahnweiler wrote of Gris seeking emblems to "recreate the reality which he imagined, deprived of all incidentals, of any imitative recollection of the emotion in which it had its origin."[69] Here, then, is *the* guitar and concept of music in archetypal, monumental terms.

The sense of a synthesizing hand that prevails in *Guitar on a Table* is present in *The Breakfast Table* (cat. 37), also painted in October 1915. The clearly stated, three-pronged compositional structure, recalling the stripes

The Pot of Geraniums, 1915 (cat. 35)

Fantômas, 1915 (cat. 36)

The Bottle of Claret, 1915 (fig. 15)

73

Guitar on a Table, 1915 (cat. 38)

The Breakfast Table, 1915 (cat. 37)

A Henriette Reverdy
amicalement
Juan Gris

Sur la table il y avait quelques grains de poudre
ou de café. La guerre ou le repos ; mais pourquoi
tout ensemble ? L'odeur nous guidait le soir plus
que nos yeux et le moulin broyait du noir, dans
nos têtes. Pourquoi les levez-vous en remuant les
lèvres ? Le voisin connaîtra vos pensées.

3

Coffee Grinder, Cup, and Glass on a Table, 1915 (cat. 91)

Fig. 16
Still Life with Poem, 1915
Oil on canvas
80.6 x 64.8 cm. (31¾ x 25½ in.)
Norton Simon Foundation, Pasadena
(DC 152)

Fig. 17   Francisco de Zurbarán
Saint Serapion, 1628
Oil on canvas
121.2 x 104.3 cm. (47¾ x 41 in.)
Wadsworth Atheneum, Hartford
The Ella Sumner and Mary Catlin
Sumner Collection

of 1913, delimits most representational incidents. The blue plane is flat, whereas its wood-grained opposite offers a plunge into depth. Between is a plane that includes both flat and plastic elements, a contrast that is echoed by the juxtaposition of the newspaper and fruit bowl.

A companion to *The Breakfast Table* is *Still Life with Poem*, 1915 (fig. 16). Rather than being poised in juxtaposition, the planes are piled one over the other in the latter work. Sculptural qualities abound, for as one plane succeeds the other, they move out toward the viewer, vying with the objects as to which projects furthest. Although the red border almost holds all in check, the table extends beyond it. The winner in this "competition" is the poem which is, in *trompe l'oeil* fashion, tacked at the lower edge as, for example, in Zurbarán's *Saint Serapion* (fig. 17). Again, Gris distinguishes the Cubist milieu, an imaginary and artful realm, from the "real" world, as shown in this case by a sheet of paper on which appears a poem by Pierre Reverdy.

Gris's poetic outlook evolved still further in 1915 when he prepared works to accompany his friend Reverdy's volume entitled *Au soleil du plafond*.[70] Gris initially intended that *Coffee Grinder, Cup, and Glass on a Table*, 1915 (cat. 91), be the frontispiece. The Reverdy poem that is in this case literally attached to the picture illustrates the kind of poetic manipulation current in Gris's milieu:

> On the cloth were a few grains of powder or coffee. War or respite
> on fronts which wrinkle together. The fragrance mingled with the calls
> of evening, the world closes its eyes and the mill ground black like our
> heads. In the circle of voices, a cloud rises. A pane of glass at the
> lip that muddles our thoughts.[71]

In Reverdy's poems, there is a continuous conflation of objects, as flat entities or as richly evocative presences in dramatic interaction. The objects have an effect quite similar to what is found in the poetry of Mallarmé, whom, Kahnweiler reports, Gris worshipped.[72] Mallarmé wanted to "describe not the object itself but the effect it produces."[73] Poets of this form depended on the object, much as the Cubist painters did.[74]

The implements of the arts are key motifs in Reverdy's poetry, just as Gris's planned insignia for the volume joins a palette and a book.[75] Reverdy's poetry is replete with metaphors and metaphoric situations that he shared with Gris. Among the titles of his poems are "The Book," "The Pipe," "The Musician," "The Guitar," "The Violin," "The Compote Dish," and "Draught Board," all themes with some history in Gris's painting. Indeed, Reverdy's titles could be used as a catalogue of Gris's favorite objects. "Signs" are everywhere, replacing words as signals and embodiments. Space is understood metaphorically, and frequently there is a comparison between here and there and constriction and relief. Reverdy was much concerned with surfaces and what lay behind them,[76] "the mystery of doors,"[77] and the unveiling potential of windows. "Musician" is typical of these interests:

> *The shadow, the musician, the immense blue curtain that parts space. It is his name that strikes the clapper, it's the air that slides along better. Seated on the deep slope of a hill, between hollowed out walls, I hear the signs run faster than my eyes. Between the walls, in front of the sky, the window in the middle, the feet on the rug where the sparks go out, or the stars, or some other luminous signs.*[78]

Underlying the fusion of objects and the multiple meanings of the words in Reverdy's poetry is a conflict or dilemma like the one intimated in the open window theme. "Against the wall, the worried author who watches the world live and doesn't follow."[79] The writer/musician in Reverdy's poems has, instead of the world, the vehicle of leaves of paper, walls, marble, or sheet music, which are planes where signs appear.[80] Within a circumscribed, interior space, Reverdy seeks some degree of tranquility "between four walls and on the table."[81] Lamps abound in his poetry, providing solace and humanity in these contained spaces. And circles have a magical presence in an otherwise difficult world. Gris's art shares many points of reference with Reverdy's poetry. Most important, for both, the allusive significance of the objects is critical to the refined play of plastic, poetic, and metaphorical manipulations.

Gris had been experimenting with object essences from late 1912, and no doubt it was he who influenced Reverdy, not vice versa. But Gris's work with the poet produced a further impetus in that direction. At this time he wanted his pictures to shed their coldness and assume "that sensitive and sensuous side which I feel should always be there."[82] The watercolors accompanying the 1915 collaboration and the contemporaneous paintings concluded in a series dated early 1916 in which objects have a heightened, immanent presence and there is a lush, pointillist surface. In *Fruit Dish and Bottle*, 1916 (cat. 41), circular and semicircular forms act theoretically as openings, yet have a bold, abstract quality. The pointillist works after Reverdy have that inspired lightness and sensuousness seen earlier in *The Pot of Geraniums* but are now formed with the system of overlapping planes that Gris evolved in the second half of 1915. An added element is the stippling with which Gris animates various surfaces. Cooper speaks of the "ventilation" that ensues,[83] a quality that aerates the otherwise constricted still lifes of this period.[84] In contrast to his contemporary pictures, Gris eliminates three-dimensional touches in favor of a constant assertion of the plane. Even the blacks, ostensibly shadows behind, are

Fruit Dish and Bottle, 1916 (cat. 41)

The Newspaper, 1916 (cat. 39)

Newspaper and Fruit Dish, 1916 (cat. 40)

locked on the surface, and there is much folding over of planes upon themselves. In sum, the pictures are virtually abstract, with Reverdy-like emblems providing the barest clues of identity and the only excuses for drawing.

Shifts in color emphasis are echoed by the mood swings described in Gris's letters. At one point during the war, he blithely declared, "My feet are anchored in pre-war times."[85] Yet only shortly thereafter he reported, "You can't imagine the feelings of gloom and disgust to which I have been prey for some time now. . . . Sometimes these periods last for weeks, sometimes for months."[86] It is not clear whether Gris considered pre-war times so happy, or if he was simply trying to remain oblivious to the war. Certainly he was concerned, constantly inquiring in letters about the state of his friends; also, Kahnweiler's exile had a great impact on him. At any rate, it is quite startling to consider the shift in palette, again, in pictures subsequent to the pointillist ones, including *The Siphon* (cat. 43) and *Hot Water Jug and Bowl* (cat. 44), both 1916.

Fruit Dish, Glass, and Lemon, 1916 (cat. 47), shows the remarkable degree to which Gris could manage black and white. His black is shadow, but it is schematically flattened, taking its place as a planar entity lying next to, not behind, the object whose reflection it is. Gris's black has many precedents in the art of his native Spain, yet his is as awesome as any in that country's history. White has the character of objectified light, as if a schematic rendering of the place where light is striking or reflecting. In the midst of these powerful contrasts appear the gold of the lemon and the rust color of the table.

Though ostensibly opposed in feeling, many of the works of this period reveal a common concern with the subject of light. It is either seen through a window, radiantly permeating a still life, or schematically present in a dark interior. Gris's fascination with light may have several sources and aspects. In Spanish Baroque still life, a metaphysical light provides illumination: "Objects thus appear to be caught between the impenetrable background and the full glare of light—rooted to the spot . . . and revealed in all their beauty."[87] Witnessing such objects becomes a "hallucinatory" experience.[88] Reverdy, too, focused great attention on a revelatory light, which is conveyed by the lamp. In his *Le gant de crin*, light allowed by a lamp or open window undoes the obscurity found in artworks and is a critical tool of the artist. As an antidote for the airtight, impervious world of art, Reverdy prescribes light, symbolizing the realm of nature.[89] Gris seems to have shared this requirement that light be present, because when he turned in 1917 to the dark, intense series of still lifes painted on panel, he retained the dramatic white highlights.

In *Bottle and Fruit Dish*, 1917 (cat. 50), the black-and-white contrast in the center imparts a dramatic struggle between the forces of light and darkness. Later in the year, Gris tended to eliminate the placid, planar

The Siphon, 1916 (cat. 43)

Hot Water Jug and Bowl, 1916 (cat. 44)

Fruit Dish, Glass, and Lemon, 1916 (cat. 47)

Water Bottle and Newspaper, 1916 (cat. 45)

Fruit Dish, Glass, and Newspaper, 1916 (cat. 46)

Still Life (Bottle and Fruit Dish), 1917 (cat. 50)

setting of such still lifes. The interior world is, thereby, made more claustrophobic, as in *Bottle and Glass*, 1917 (cat. 51). Again verging toward abstraction, Gris could say of a picture like this that it "resembled nothing, no object, no real-life scene."[90] Instead, a relieflike surface full of energy and complexity is formed.[91] There is not the least hint of an ingratiating aspect, as had appeared in *The Pot of Geraniums*, 1915 (cat. 35). One culmination to this tendency is *Still Life with Plaque*, 1917 (cat. 54). Though the whites represent light, their presence is shrill. With neither air nor depth, Gris creates an abstract, cohesive surface, one that even spreads beyond to the *trompe-l'oeil* frame. His white is equally abstract and theoretical; in Reverdy's sense, it conceptually provides the light of nature in an otherwise airless setting.

Simultaneous with still lifes in which objects are reduced to signs or disappear are several pictures that are virtually portraits of objects. Léger is sometimes given credit, in certain works of 1924–25, for predicting "object-painting," that is, the isolation of an object against a planar composition.[92] Yet Gris precedes him by a number of years. Though he had shown an early interest in manufactured objects, Gris reserved his greatest emotion and energy for tools of musicians. These possess heightened, idealized connotations for Gris and are worthy of his greatest efforts. But his aim was synthetic. He wrote of wanting "to create new objects which cannot be compared with any objects in reality. . . . My *Violin*, being a creation, need fear no comparison."[93] He wanted a synthetic creation of the mind, not an imitation of nature. Among his highest achievements in this regard is *The Violin*, 1916 (fig. 18). The composition, as usual based on overlapping color planes, harmonizes diagonal, vertical, and horizontal thrusts, transparencies, solids, and voids. Static and ghostly, isolated and hieratic, the instrument is the summation of Gris's emotions before this object. It is more than an object-emblem or an accumulation of aspects; it is, rather, a personal metaphor, like the guitar. Near the end of his career Gris would make explicit what was implicit in his art, that the musical instrument, as a tool of the musician, was an analogue to the implements of the painter. A majesty exists in this work that represents Gris at his finest.

As if in response, Gris painted a second *Violin* (cat. 48) one month later. This one is another instrument altogether, not only in "pose" but in stature. Perhaps a clue is the absence of the sheet music, normally the attribute of the archetypal instrument. Instead, we find the object as motif, analyzed plastically. Here Gris seems to present the "object-emblem," for the emphasis is on the sound hole as an identity-clue: the formal analysis and breakup of the violin supercedes its grandeur of a month earlier. Gris seeks to integrate the object in space as if it were an element of a still life. The blacks are especially striking, seeming to bend any recession back to the surface plane.

Fig. 18 (See p. 92)
The Violin, 1916
Oil on plywood
116.5 x 73 cm. (45¾ x 28¼ in.)
Kunstmuseum Basel
(DC 184)

Still Life (Bottle and Glass), 1917 (cat. 51)

Guitar, Glass, and Water Bottle, 1917 (cat. 53)

The Violin, 1916 (fig. 18)

The Violin, 1916 (cat. 48)

Fig. 19
Woman with a Mandolin, after Corot, 1916
Oil on plywood
92 x 60 cm. (36¼ x 23⅝ in.)
Kunstmuseum Basel
(DC 197)

Fig. 20   Jean-Baptiste Camille Corot
Girl with a Mandolin, 1860–65
Oil on canvas
51.4 x 36.8 cm. (20¼ x 14½ in.)
The Saint Louis Art Museum

At about the same time as *The Violin*, Gris painted his first human portraits in several years. Before the familiar wainscoting that is the setting for the Basel *Violin*, Gris placed his own *Self-portrait*, 1916 (cat. 42). Absent is the humor of the figures of 1912–13; Gris shows the intense gloom about which he remarked in his letter. Shortly after, he painted a companion, half-length image of Josette, which he then turned into the full-length *Portrait of Josette Gris*, 1916 (cat. 49). The relationship of Gris's *Self-portrait* to the subsequent *Portrait of Josette* is similar to that of the first violin to the second. That is, the first of each pair has the quality of a psychological rendering whereas the second is more pictorial.

Surely one of Gris's greatest achievements, the *Portrait of Josette* is based on his studies after Corot (fig. 19) and Cézanne (cat. 92).[94] He magnificently integrates foreground and background elements on one plane. This feat is accomplished primarily through color rhythms that unite differing spatial planes. The blacks, employed to signify bosom, derrière, and leg, as well as the prominent shadow of the figure, all occupy places on the forward plane. Transparency does not result in an illusion of depth but instead becomes another means of joining planes of the picture. The composition is a dynamic medley of pictorial elements.

A critical turning point for Gris was his *Woman with a Mandolin, after Corot*, 1916 (figs. 19 and 20), yet its importance may have been as much iconographic as formal. Having dealt with himself only momentarily, and having virtually concluded the theme of the guitar and violin, he, nevertheless, still wanted a personal statement. The *Corot* painting gave him a vehicle, the player of a musical instrument. From this painting, it was a logical step for Gris to move to a male musician and the longtime theme among his colleagues, the harlequin. Early in the century, Picasso had utilized it, along with musicians and *saltimbanques*, as a surrogate of the artist. Symbolic of a marginal life, alienation, wit, and artifice, the harlequin was an archetypal hero for Picasso's "gang." Picasso returned once more to the subject beginning late in 1915, but perhaps as important to Gris was Cézanne's harlequin, after which he made several studies in 1916.

Harlequin with a Guitar, 1917 (cat. 52), is the first painting devoted to the male musician-harlequin following his drawn studies of Cézanne's harlequin (cat. 92) and the *Corot* of the preceding year. Just as in the *Corot*, the primary three-dimensional emphases are on the head, fingers, and fret in *Harlequin with a Guitar*. Gris did not always include the musical attribute of the harlequin in his many subsequent renderings of the figure. This work records the critical moment when his iconography shifted. The picture is much in the spirit of the still lifes of late 1917, for there is great complexity and dynamic equilibrium. The result is activation of the entire surface, with essentially no depth indicated. The virtuosity of this work signals a new, more consistent stylistic phase of Gris's career.

Portrait of Josette Gris, 1916 (cat. 49)

Head of a Harlequin, after Cézanne, 1916 (cat. 92)

Harlequin with a Guitar, 1917 (cat. 52)

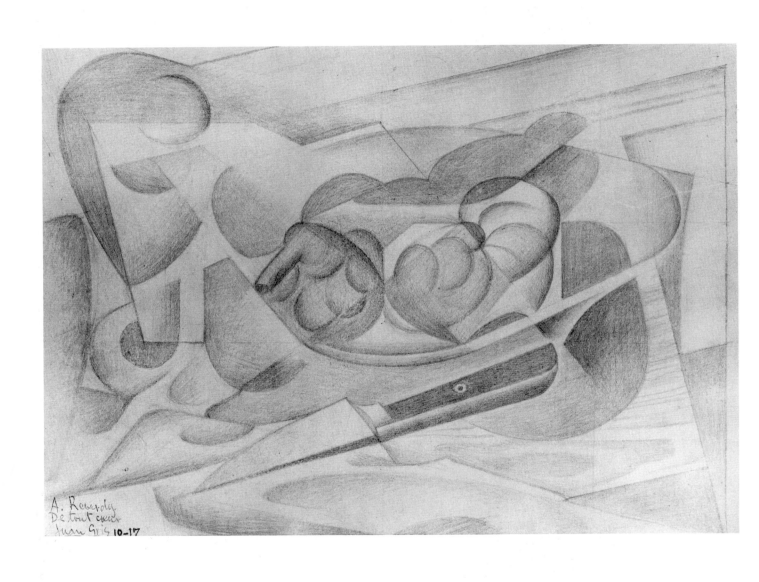

Still Life with Knife, 1917 (cat. 93)

The Guitar, 1918 (cat. 57)

Still Life with Plaque, 1917 (cat. 54)

Synthesis: 1918 to mid-1922

The period immediately following the war was the most consistent of Gris's career. During this time he often achieved an utterly fluid interpenetration of pictorial structure with incidents of an observed reality. In so doing, he became the leader, in effect, of a movement known as "Cubist-classicism."[95] Among the Classicists were André Lhote, Jean Metzinger, Gino Severini, Diego Rivera, and Jacques Lipchitz. Most were showing at the gallery of Léonce Rosenberg, along with Gris who had joined Rosenberg because of Kahnweiler's exile.

The classic mode of Cubism began to emerge in 1916–17 and became consolidated as a group style about 1918. It reached its peak upon becoming the movement called "Purism," the leaders of which were Amédée Ozenfant and Charles Jeanneret (Le Corbusier). With his methodical approach, as distinguished from the intuitive outlook of Picasso, Gris was a beacon for the Classicists and Purists, as he had been earlier for the *Section d'or* group. The aim of the Classicists was an art based on rational proportions and abstract schemes; aspects from the real world were either eliminated or minimized. By contrast, Gris always retained his respect for the object and never would turn toward pure abstraction, as did his contemporaries.[96] For that reason, he was never truly one of the Classicists or Purists in a substantive sense. Indeed, he tended to find fault with their periodical, *Nord-Sud*, and even its editor, Reverdy.[97]

Gris continued to refer to the "poetic" aspect of his work during this period. With the reciprocal relationship of structure to object, his compositions could yield a certain lyricism. Gris sought "an imaginary reality,"[98] a construct that can be compared to those being created by contemporary writers, including Jean Cocteau who was a friend of Gris beginning in 1916–17.[99] Cocteau wanted poetic realities in which objects have "a suspicious air."[100] In Cubist poetry, too, a kind of "natural mysticism" due to the obsessive treatment of the details of objects pervaded.[101] Whether Gris was influenced by the poets or they by him is moot. More important is that they all participated in one group, examining and discussing each others' work closely;[102] and poetic qualities were prized by all.

Guitar, Glass, and Water Bottle (cat. 53), painted in December 1917, shows the new style. No longer making portraits of objects, Gris manipulates object-emblems, their formal and identifying characteristics. In *Violin and Glass*, 1918 (cat. 56), aspects of the objects indicate what is represented yet, at once, have an abstract life. A Léger-like cone in the middle of the picture is the primary, three-dimensional touch in this otherwise flat rendering. It is symptomatic that the still life now overflows its borders onto the painted frame, for the subject cannot be neatly contained but is part of a formal arrangement integrated with the surroundings. Black and white are generally less emphatic in 1918 and 1919.

Violin and Glass, 1918 (cat. 56)

Fruit Dish and Playing Cards, 1918 (cat. 55)

Guitar and Fruit Dish, 1919 (cat. 59)

Still Life with Fruit Dish and Mandolin (fig. 21)
(Still Life with Guitar), 1919

105

Fig. 21 (See p. 105)
*Still Life with Fruit Dish and Mandolin
(Still Life with Guitar)*, 1919
Oil on canvas
92 x 65 cm. (36¼ x 25⅝ in.)
Private collection, Paris
(DC 303)

Fig. 22   Jean-Siméon Chardin
Attributes of the Arts, 1765
Oil on canvas
91 x 145 cm. (35⅞ x 57 1/16 in.)
Louvre, Paris

Works such as *Guitar and Fruit Dish* (cat. 59) and *Still Life with Fruit Dish and Mandolin* (fig. 21) show Gris reaching a high pitch of virtuosity and complexity in 1919. The eye jumps across an undulating surface of details. Much balancing and rhyming of elements occurs, for example between the strings of an instrument and the lines of sheet music. Representationally, the energy is almost carried into the viewer's space by the corner of a table being placed at the lower edge of the picture. But unlike earlier work in which this device is utilized, the objects are not tipped forward from the table but are firmly locked on the pictorial plane.

In the latter half of 1919 and in early 1920—in *Guitar and Fruit Dish* (cat. 59), and *Fruit Dish and Newspaper*, 1920 (cat. 63), for instance— Gris greatly simplified his compositions while achieving a dynamic equilibrium between representation and abstraction. An object is presented by a minimal sign, and that sign has significance as a component in an overall harmony. Rhyming on the flat plane is a major characteristic of this clarified realm. Blacks again play an important role in these lyrical works as "fossils of shading."[103] At this time, Gris's influence was considerable not only on the Classicists and Purists, but even on Braque.[104] Indeed, from this time forward, Gris's position as a spokesman for Cubism was consolidated.

Gris returned to the more complex vision of early 1919 later the following year, but having learned certain lessons. Instead of showing the corner of a table leaning into the viewer's space, he now rendered it parallel to the picture plane or as an abstract surface. He resumed a more overt system of proportions, generally using a ratio of three to five as a means of relating parts to each other and to the overall format. His objects became united with these pictorial structures and at this time he often seemed to begin with an "architectural" idea of the picture. Compositions with an underlying structure based on an *M* are common,[105] and his favorite, the triangle, is often present.[106] Such developments resulted in some of his most elegant still lifes, including *Guitar, Pipe, and Sheets of Music* (cat. 64), *Guitar and Clarinet* (cat. 65), and *Guitar and Fruit Dish* (cat. 66), all 1920; *Guitar and Fruit Dish*, 1921 (cat. 69); and *The Book of Music*, 1922 (cat. 71).

Meyer Schapiro writes of the importance of recognizing the artist's choices for representation in a still life because these show qualities of the artist's thinking and personality.[107] This process is especially revealing in Gris's case. He favored objects that reflect human activity, instead of such traditional motifs as fruit and flowers; the human condition is, therefore, implied. His choices developed from his love and knowledge of the old masters (cf. fig. 22). Hence, in works from this period, the selection has a quite allegorical sense. Books suggest poetry, instruments posit music, and the picture plane itself, on which transformations occur, is a metaphor of painting. Beside the arts, Gris added elements traditionally indicative

Fruit Dish and Newspaper, 1920 (cat. 63)

Still Life, 1920 (cat. 96)

Guitar and Clarinet, 1920 (cat. 65)

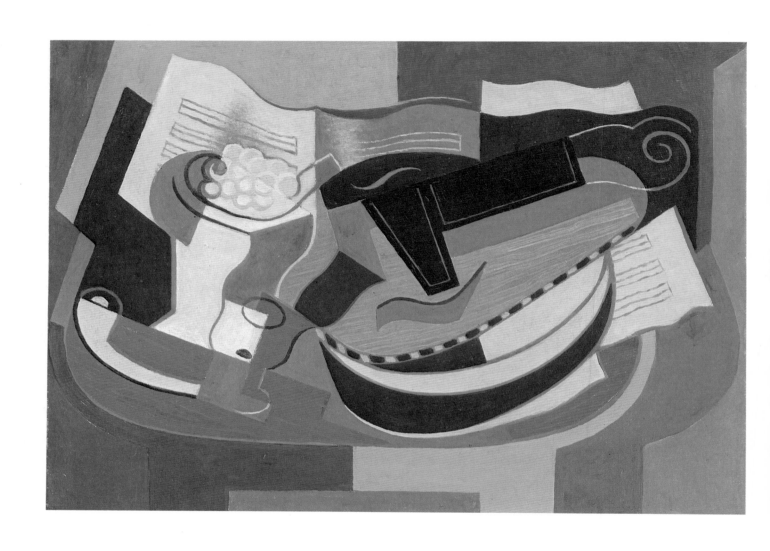

Guitar and Fruit Dish, 1920 (cat. 66)

Guitar and Fruit Dish, 1921 (cat. 69)

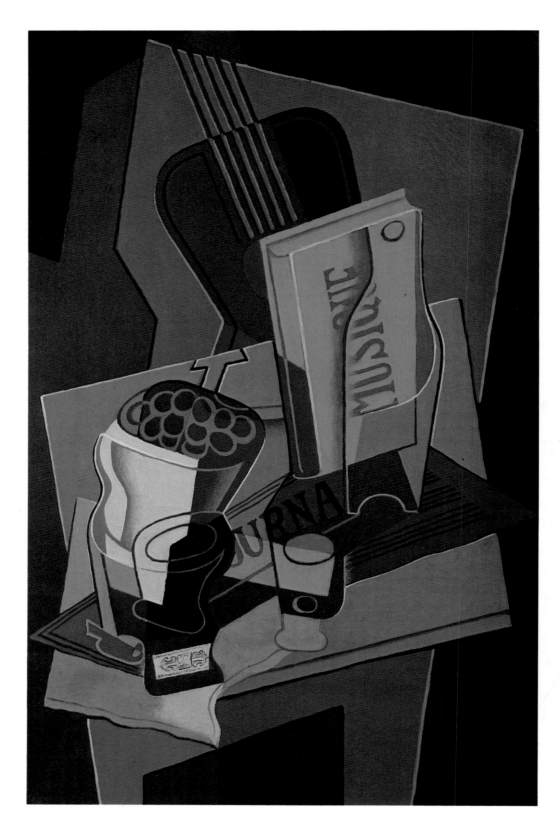

The Book of Music, 1922 (cat. 71)

Fig. 23
The Miller, 1918
Oil on canvas
100 x 81 cm. (39⅜ x 31⅞ in.)
Private collection
(DC 263)

Fig. 24
The Touraine Peasant, 1918
Oil on plywood
100 x 65 cm. (39⅜ x 25⅝ in.)
Musée National d'Art Moderne,
Centre Georges Pompidou, Paris
(DC 282)

of the senses, such as grapes, pipes, and playing cards. Yet, just as he was never a mindless follower of Picasso and Braque, Gris also invented new combinations of conventional, allegorical attributes. Rarely did he record the symbols of all five senses in one work. Rather, he composed objects that epitomize a basic dichotomy which can be variously stated: life versus art; the sensuous versus the intellectual; the anecdotal versus the sublime.

A poetic turn of mind is also present in Gris's rendering of figures between 1918 and 1922. Although "classicizing figuration" was everywhere apparent in Paris,[108] Gris's figures, as discussed earlier, had not only formal but meaningful content. Though generally seeking unity of figure and ground in *The Miller* (fig. 23) and *The Touraine Peasant* (fig. 24), both 1918, he juxtaposed the space occupied by the figures with an implied realm, up the stairs or through the door. This second, mysterious world has a shadowy guardian in both pictures. In the first, a head is made part of the steps, while a similar profile appears at the lower right corner of the door in the second work. Both may be construed as wittily defined spirits of the unseen realm or as disconnected and metamorphosed shadows of the larger figures.[109]

Gris wrote while painting *Peasant*, "I'm immersed in a dream about such important work that I think of nothing else. Time and space only exist in my life as ideas or as elements of my work."[110] By virtue of the doors in *Peasant* and *Miller*, Gris implies movement through time and space. Through these doors are other spaces, as well as either a future or a past time. The present is given by the depiction of the figures. A similar principle is applicable in Gris's contemporary still lifes in that the rhythms and manipulations constantly direct us through space and time.

The harlequins of 1919 possess the same mysterious yet mechanical quality as the figures of the preceding year. Double visages are present in *Harlequin at Table* (cat. 58) and *Harlequin with Guitar* (cat. 60). Unexplained in the first is the yellow "shadow" of a hat not shown on the figure's head. And, again, there is a second being present, in the head on the right edge and the hands on the opposite side. Perhaps Gris's aspiration to synthesize a number of spaces and times in one work explains these hallucinatory presences. These figurative works, as opposed to *Miller* and *Peasant*, demonstrate a more complete integration of figure and ground. Abstract planes are at once representational details. Rhyming of color and form reaches a particularly exquisite pitch in *Harlequin at Table*.

It is often asserted that by 1919 Gris started all his works with an abstract formula and then made the object or figure fit. Yet comparison of a rare preparatory study (cat. 95) to the finished painting shows that Gris, in fact, abstracted a representational idea. On the other hand, *Pierrot*, 1922 (cat. 72), exhibits a simpler, planar arrangement, as opposed to the transparencies of *Harlequin at Table*. As in the still lifes of this time, such as

Study for "Harlequin with Guitar," 1919 (cat. 95)

Harlequin with Guitar, 1919 (cat. 60)

Harlequin at Table, 1919 (cat. 58)

Pierrot, 1922 (cat. 72)

Fig. 25
The Open Window, 1917
Oil on panel
100 x 72.8 cm. (39⅜ x 28⅝ in.)
Philadelphia Museum of Art
The Louise and Walter Arensberg Collection
(DC 219)

Fig. 26   Henri Matisse
The Violinist at the Window, 1917–18
Oil on canvas
150 x 98 cm. (59 x 38½ in.)
Musée National d'Art Moderne,
Centre Georges Pompidou, Paris

The Book of Music, the figure is presented as whole, rather than fragmented. The character of this pierrot is emphatically stated. It assumes a defiant, warriorlike stance that supercedes its existence as a motif.

Gris's drawn portraits of this period seem an outlet for another side of his creativity. They reveal an emphasis on the character and bearing of the individuals. The visages of Madame Lipchitz, 1918 (cat. 94), Kahnweiler (cat. 97), Madame Leiris (cat. 98), and himself (cat. 99), all 1921, demonstrate Gris's enormous linear virtuosity, as well as his ever-present love of plastically rendered forms.

The sense of the poetic that Gris ascribed to this phase of his work is most apparent in pictures in which the guitar is isolated before an open window. These juxtapositions and/or syntheses of interior and exterior worlds are preceded, first, by *Place Ravignan*, 1915, where Gris compared a still life in a constricted interior with a dreamy exterior on the same plane. In *The Open Window*, 1917 (fig. 25), the airy exterior world completely envelopes the room. Although the viewer is theoretically within, he/she is very close to the window. Notable in both works is the door which, like the windows, is a threshold to the spacious, magical realm beyond. Gris picks up this personal theme again in 1921, and it continues until the end of his life.

Living beside the sea at Bandol in 1921, Gris had diverse reactions to the setting. It was "sinister," "beautiful," and "sad."[111] So moved was he that the theme of the open window dominated his production that year. In the first of these works, *The Open Window*, 1921 (cat. 67), Gris returned to the metaphoric conception of *Place Ravignan*. That is, the interior and exterior spaces are distinct. Instead of a still life before a window, however, Gris discovered an archetypical subject for him, the musical instrument before nature. Though no text exists to make this combination a conventionally recognized allegory, the two principal components have long traditions in art history and in Gris's own evolution. We may, thus, speak of a private system of symbols in this case.[112] Again, Gris's friendship with Matisse may have intervened, for until the latter's paintings of 1917 (fig. 26), an instrument before a window did not exist in the history of the window motif in art,[113] although it was hinted at in allegories of the senses.[114] The interior, characterized by music, is evocative of the human world of art and intellect. The landscape has direct, visual, and sensuous qualities typical of nature. There is perhaps implicit a yearning for that natural simplicity. Potential for a merger is shown by the rhythmic repetition of curves in the guitar and mountains and in the cloud that begins to enter the room.

Later in the year a pictorial-poetic synthesis is achieved in *The View across the Bay* (cat. 68). Like *Open Window* of 1917, the interior and exterior interpenetrate. The synthesis is partly accomplished in both works

The Open Window, 1921 (cat. 67)

Still Life (Guitar, Pipe, and Sheets of Music), 1920 (cat. 64)

Portrait of Madame Lipchitz, 1918 (cat. 94)

Guitar and Fruit Dish, 1919 (cat. 61)

Guitar, Book, and Newspaper, 1920 (cat. 62)

by the rhythmic relationship of rectangles. Also, the table is forced up into the window opening so that the objects appear to be on water and on the table at once. Most evocative is the triangular sail of a boat sitting on the table. The guitar, too, is made part of the natural, watery realm, as it was in the *Minstrel's Soul* fifteen years earlier. And the rhyming of curves between the guitar and mountains is especially direct now. The scene and the objects within have an apparitional quality created partly by the sense of airiness. Gris turns that quality into a joke and makes comic the achievement of synthesizing interior and exterior with the words LE PET, which is the French slang equivalent of "fart."

Notwithstanding his jokes, Gris continued to elaborate the theme of the open window in 1921, concluding with *The Mountain "Le Canigou"* (cat. 70) painted at Céret in December. In it he returned to the juxtaposition of interior and exterior as separate and distinct. Whereas a sail became a triangle in the previously discussed work, the mountain now assumes that form, much as it had for Wassily Kandinsky and Paul Klee starting about 1910.[115] Although there is no reason to believe that Gris knew of the works and writings from Munich, it is a remarkable coincidence to find him manipulating this favorite form of the Blaue Reiter artists in a similar manner. Perhaps Cézanne lies at the heart of these usages.[116] At any rate, by making the mountain triangular and regularizing the form of the guitar, he was rendering the poetic juxtaposition in terms of object-emblems. Diagrammatic, too, is nature, as a blue rectangle containing the triangular mountain and the white swatch of cloud. Opposed are the curved lines of the guitar. It and an open book epitomize art. As usual, the door is present as both a barrier and a means of entry.

Although creating some of his finest paintings in 1921 and early 1922, Gris was plagued by doubts and questions regarding acceptance of his work, sales, and whether he was receiving adequate attention. Adding to his woes, the first symptoms of serious illness occurred in May 1920, and these barely relented for the rest of his life. He and Josette were forced to move frequently in search of a climate that would prove beneficial.

The View across the Bay, 1921 (cat. 68)

The Mountain "Le Canigou," 1921 (cat. 70)

Retreat then Resolution: Mid-1922 to 1927

In works from mid-1922 through 1924, there is a discernible falling off in the quality of Gris's work. For approximately three years he seemed to suffer a lapse in his resolve and to retreat from the course he had been pursuing. His usual passion for clarity and form is absent. Instead, his art is filled with tentative, confused still lifes and sentimental or sometimes comic figures. The period is marked, too, by health problems, especially asthma and uremia, and the psychological doubts mentioned at the end of the last chapter. This is also the time of his frequent commissions for Diaghilev's ballet company in 1923–24.

Gris's work with the ballet necessitated long sojourns in Monte Carlo. Although he had no interest in the work itself, disliked Monte Carlo, and resented these experiences, he felt compelled to accept the offers. Through these he hoped to gain some of the attention he felt was due him. Perhaps for the same reasons, he accepted several commissions to do book illustrations in 1924. But he gained no great acclaim as a result; rather, these experiences merely served to divert him further from his usual pursuits. Indeed the work for the ballet was only a modest success in his own evaluation, and the conventional style Gris adopted for his work with Diaghilev may even have altered his vision somewhat.

Certainly other factors must have contributed to the years of retreat. In late 1922 and early 1923 Gris would have noticed Picasso shifting to his classical phase and also creating a great deal of work for Diaghilev. That Picasso was for the moment backing away from Cubism was only one aspect of a general questioning of the Cubist aesthetic occurring then. In April 1922 in a pamphlet entitled *Le coeur à barbe: Journal transparent*, Tristan Tzara felt the need to rebut Dada claims that Cubism was dead. More talk of the demise of Cubism occurred in 1923.[117] In the meantime, Purism was turning Cubism toward a more emphatic purity than Gris had ever wanted. At the opposite extreme, Surrealism, with its greater stress on the unconscious than on pictorial values, was gaining adherents. Adding to these conflicting directions, Gris was reading a great deal of mystical literature at the time.[118]

Gris painted a number of works utilizing a figurative or harlequin theme in these years. Often the ghost of Corot's *Girl with a Mandolin* (fig. 20) seems present in the downturned, melancholic eyes. These renderings rarely show Gris's familiar pictorial strength built of Cubist synthesis. Instead, a kind of expressionist naturalism is generally employed, and at times the artist appears influenced by the Amarna style of Egyptian art in the elongated, distorted proportions and faces of the figures. The harlequins and pierrots often assume narrative poses, stare awkwardly out at the viewer (fig. 27), or are shown in utterly resigned and vulnerable positions. Open windows continue as symbols of idle yearning. The pathos that fills

Fig. 27
Harlequin Leaning on a Table, 1924
Oil on canvas
92 x 73 cm. (36¼ x 28¾ in.)
Bayerische Staatsgemäldesammlungen, Munich
(DC 494)

these works must be related to Gris's own mental state.

One of the few impressive pictures from the period of mid-1922 through 1924 is *Seated Harlequin*, 1923 (cat. 73), in which Gris's familiar ability to integrate two- and three-dimensional aspects is present. The figure has a totemic quality and is devoid of the sentiment in most contemporaneous works, such as *Woman with Scarf*, 1924 (cat. 74).

Although Gris had for all practical purposes made a retreat, he nevertheless accomplished certain advances. He had always been fond of debating problems of art.[119] At this time, he put his theories in writing, publishing "Notes on My Painting" in 1923. Then in 1924 he delivered a lecture at the Sorbonne to the Society of Philosophical and Scientific Studies. Entitled "On the Possibilities of Painting," the paper was subsequently published in French, German, Spanish, and English. In these writings, Gris articulated and asserted the Cubist aesthetic at the very moment that it was under attack. As a result he found a considerable audience and gained a certain attention, both of which had eluded him in his role as a Cubist painter.

In his writings, Gris describes his "deductive" method, whereby "it is not picture 'X' which manages to correspond with my subject, but subject 'X' which manages to correspond with my picture."[120] He also describes the "architecture" of a painting, as well as various pictorial issues.[121] Yet, in spite of the frequently remarked clarity of these essays, Gris was, at the very moment of writing, experiencing a crisis over the principles he was articulating and, indeed, was contradicting them in his work. Moreover, these principles, which appeared to be lucid and well-founded in his previous practice, are, in fact, given exaggerated emphasis in the writing. The contradictions are apparent when his words are carefully reviewed in relation to his earlier statements, letters, overall *oeuvre*, and comments by close friends at earlier moments in his career. For instance, he claimed to disdain plasticity, but this quality was present throughout his career. He asserted that his subjects simply suggested themselves through pictorial relationships, a claim that often guides writers on Gris. Yet he quite obviously and intentionally repeated the same subjects over and over. While rejecting symbolism, he asserted the necessity of worthwhile subject matter in the creation of great art. Although imbued with this heightened sense of the subject's importance, he failed to articulate his method of poetic metaphor in these credolike essays. Perhaps the reason for these contradictions regarding subject matter is that he was depressed by the sentiment in his contemporaneous works. In order to purge this aspect for himself, it was necessary to take an overly formalistic approach in these didactic writings. And certainly the exercise worked. It seems that as the result of having articulated some basic ideas, Gris was strengthened mentally and managed to resume his pictorial development in 1925.

Seated Harlequin, 1923 (cat. 73)

Woman with Scarf, 1924 (cat. 74)

The last years of Gris's life, from 1925 to 1927, were filled with physical pain. His various problems produced conflicting and probably inaccurate diagnoses.[122] Although suffering, he rarely complained, but he was forced to relocate frequently, always in search of the proper clime for his failing health. Special diets and immobility caused him to lead what he called a "monastic" life wherever he was in residence.[123] Ironically, during these final years he gained a great deal more recognition, but this attention probably resulted most from his role as a spokesman for Cubism.

The Blue Cloth, 1925 (cat. 75), shows the magnificent virtuosity Gris could muster in these last years. The painting is a study in rhythmic curves, which are otherwise rare in his entire career. Movement and energy are virtually unceasing on the canvas, even in the flat corner areas defined by curves. So vibrant is the picture that it has an abstract quality. But, in fact, the objects are more or less whole.

If *The Blue Cloth* is about curved lines, *The Open Book*, 1925 (cat. 76), is a tour de force in angularity. And whereas in the former, Gris basically maintains the picture plane, in the latter, there is considerable contrast between two- and three-dimensional shapes. Indeed, the profusion seems to fall forward from the picture. Juxtaposing a book, a musical instrument, and grapes has an allegorical tone once more. But allegorical dichotomies are made into syntheses by Gris's poetic-pictorial method. That is, experiences of sight, sound, and taste are joined in a composition of intellectual and physical pleasure.

A leitmotif of the period is the palette, which had personal associations for Gris as early as 1906 in his illustrations for *Alma América* (fig. 28). On this image alone, among the dozens in the book, Gris had chosen to sign his name. Adding to the import of this moment in Gris's life was the title of the chapter—"En el Museo del Prado"—and the likelihood that this was probably the first time Gris used his new pseudonym. Thus the artist had announced himself to the world with his attribute, the palette; his new name, J. Gris; and his aspiration to join the masters in the Prado. In subsequent years, the palette appears in the *Portrait of Picasso* but was otherwise absent from his iconography. Instead, musical instruments served a parallel role. But in Gris's last years, the palette returned. With it, Gris evoked the visual arts specifically, suggesting a certain grandeur to them; and when he combined the palette with a musical instrument,[124] or a book,[125] conveyed a meaningful analogy of artist's tools.

In *The Painter's Window*, 1925 (cat. 77), Gris collected some of his favorite motifs: the palette, guitar, pipe, fruit, and playing cards. These symbols of the senses appear before an open window. But instead of the opening unveiling a tempting, sought-after world, it simply juxtaposes the other side of the interior-exterior relationship. *The Musician's Table*, 1926 (cat. 78), shows a now-familiar allegorical subject, but with certain

Fig. 28   Illustration from *Alma América, Poemas indoespañoles*, by José Santos Chocano, 1906, p. 51. The Museum of Modern Art, New York The Louis E. Stern Collection.

The Blue Cloth, 1925 (cat. 75)

The Open Book, 1925 (cat. 76)

The Painter's Window, 1925 (cat. 77)

The Musician's Table, 1926 (cat. 78)

additions from the visual arts. Gris included a bust, symbolic of sculpture, and the backs of some canvases. In addition, a window frame is present, which forms a visual and poetic rhyme with the stretchers of the paintings. Compared with this inventory, *The Table with the Red Cloth*, 1926 (cat. 79), is a simpler, more monumental statement. The juxtaposition of guitar and fruit at once suggests a dramatic contrast of intellect and sensuality.

In these last pictures of 1926–27, Gris sought a certain stasis and monumental statement of one of his lifelong themes—and the one that dominated his thoughts at the end of his life—the still life before an open window. The guitar, through it all, stands as an archetype of artistic activity of all kinds. *Guitar and Music Paper*, 1926 (cat. 80), reveals the theme in elemental terms. Like *Le Canigou*, the aspects are stark and symbolic, and underlying is a system of proportional relationships. Rendered in hard, geometrical forms, the objects are not fractured but whole. The window molding is the intermediate zone separating the interior world of art from the exterior realm of nature. But the outdoors are minimized again, and one seems to look through a kind of "cell" window that is in keeping with the "monastic" life Gris was then living.

The final figure Gris would create was *Woman with a Basket*, 1927 (cat. 82), which was in fact his last painting. Gris described these late personages as having a Pompeian and Ecole de Fontainebleau air in their classicism.[126] An oval window (or mirror) is now blackened, as Gris presents a somber climax to his most profoundly felt theme. Is this the artist's muse bringing him his still-life subject to paint, or an angel of death, or perhaps the final translation of his musician stationed before a window? Compare Mallarmé's "Saint":

> At the window holding
> The old cedarwood disgilt
> Of her lute shining
> Once with flute or mandola,
>
> Stands the pale saint spreading
> The old book which unfolds
> On the Magnificat glistening
> Once for vespers and compline:
>
> At this monstrance window
> Brushed by the harp that an angel
> Makes in his evening flight
> For the delicate tip

The Table with the Red Cloth, 1926 (cat. 79)

137

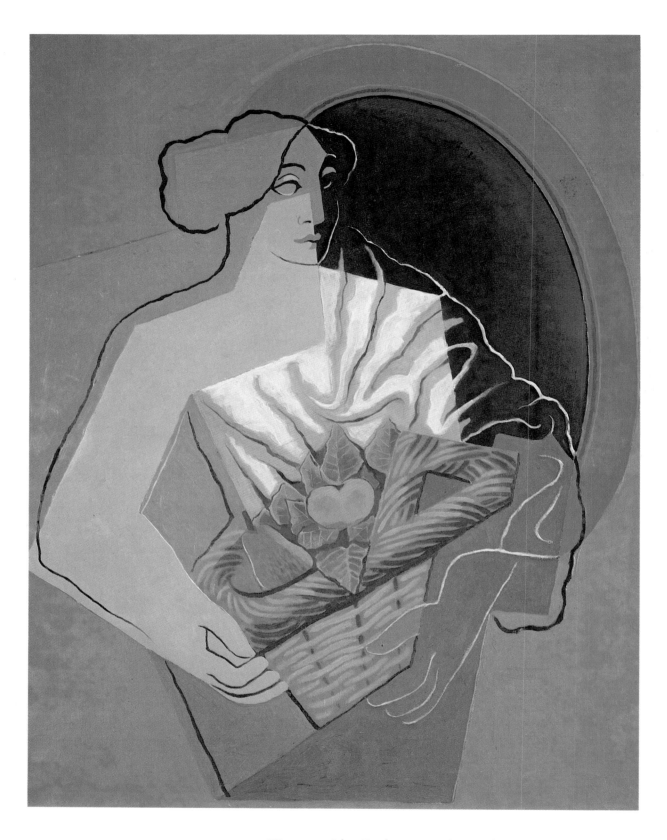

Woman with a Basket, 1927 (cat. 82)

Of the finger that without cedar
Or old book she balances
On the feathered instrument,
Musician of silence.[127]

Gris succumbed to chronic renal failure on May 11, 1927.[128] Among the mourners at his funeral were his son, Georges Gonzalez-Gris, and his friends Lipchitz, Raynal, Kahnweiler, and Picasso.

The degree to which Gris was indebted to Picasso is incalculable. From the initial learning period at Bateau Lavoir grew a kind of hero worship, and Gris often seemed to look to his countryman for guidance. His admiration was the more extreme for the overt feelings of inferiority he suffered.[129] Perhaps spitefully, Picasso added to the developing relationship by calling Gris "la fille soumise," a pun relating a subjugated daughter and registered prostitute.[130] Yet the comradely and trusting Gris did not, apparently, hold a grudge, often asking after Picasso in his letters.

Gris's reliance on Picasso did not prevent him from making an enormous contribution to Cubism. Indeed, he achieved his own voice in the Cubist pantheon, perhaps to the annoyance of Picasso. Stein reports that Gris was "the only person whom Picasso wished away."[131] The meaning of the comment must have to do with her regard for Gris. Much admired by both Spaniards for her sharp aesthetic judgment, Stein became very close with Gris. (She wrote, "We were intimate.")[132] Stein writes that as they grew close, Picasso became deeply displeased and attacked Gris's work to her.[133] The attacks had no effect, for Stein later wrote of Cubism that "Picasso created it and Juan Gris permeated it with his clarity and exaltations."[134] Undoubtedly it was to Picasso's intense jealousy that she called Gris "a perfect painter"; and in comparing the two, she remarked that Picasso had "less clarity of intellectual purpose."[135] The denouement to this unhappy triangle occurred after Gris's funeral. Stein was at home suffering the loss of Gris when Picasso came and spent the day with her. Alice B. Toklas (Stein) reports:

> I do not know what was said but I do know that at one time Gertrude Stein said to him bitterly, you have no right to mourn, and he said, you have no right to say that to me. You never realised his meaning because you did not have it, she said angrily. You know very well I did, he replied.[136]

Fruit Dish and Book, 1927 (cat. 81)

Conclusion

Just as one begins to comprehend the complexities of a canvas by Juan Gris, new qualities emerge. Especially to be noted are his extraordinarily subtle composition; great color virtuosity; passion for form; integrity and logic of approach; and ability to balance two- and three-dimensional aspects. These qualitites contribute to the nature of Gris's distinct voice in Cubism. But his reverence for the poetic quality of objects and his iconographic richness have received insufficient attention. These qualities stimulated his contemporaries to speak of him as the poetic, metaphysical, classic, or mystical Cubist.

Raynal wrote that Gris "must have a subject and it is from the subject that he makes his painting."[137] An intention of the Cubist painter, according to Raynal, is

> to conceive an object . . . to aim at knowing it in its essence, at representing it in the mind . . . as purely as possible, as a sign, as a totem *if you like.* . . . *the artist will not situate the object in a particular place, but in space, which is infinite.*[138]

These comments are appropriate, for Raynal was the closest of Gris's confidants,[139] excepting Kahnweiler. Gris and Raynal repeatedly emphasize the consequence of the subject in art. Indeed a frequent fear of the Cubists in general was the elimination of subject matter and concomitant loss of communicative power.[140] Yet there was much conflict and contradiction about how subjects were employed. Ever on guard against the literary excesses of Surrealism and other manifestations, Gris and Raynal always attacked symbolism per se. Another conflict emerged from the conventionally held Cubist view that objects, according to a Platonic ideal, should be revealed as free of experience determined by the senses. The Cubists' motivations in part derived from a disdain for anecdotalism, imitation, and the transitoriness of the Impressionists. The object as an absolute entity was the goal, revealed in a pure, essential state.[141]

Gris's idea of a poetic or, as he called it, "imaginary reality"[142] comprised an essential, plastic image of the object, free of anecdotalism, as well as an emotion with regard to that object.[143] The plastic-poetic metaphor emerged as a vehicle in this variously described poetic reality.[144] Some meaningful vehicle was necessary, for Gris clearly did not want abstraction. In fact, he wrote of wanting "to humanize" the architectural aspect of his art.[145] Gris's metaphor was the universal subject described in precise, individual terms. This transformation was the essence of Gris's deductive process, whereby he moved from the general to the particular. For example, writing about "Negro sculptures" in 1920, he admired their "individualistic representations of universal ideas,"[146] or about Christian art, he said the

Church "took the abstract idea of God and turned it into gentle Jesus. . . . It's exactly my own procedure."[147]

It is perhaps paradoxical to discover that the lifelong Cubist, Juan Gris, was not simply a formalist in the contemporary, exaggerated sense of that term. Rather, his poetic nature led him toward notions of universality and metaphor. Most ironic of all is that Gris's reverence for the object had direct implications for the Surrealists. They, too, located objects in a poetic milieu, though largely ignoring the Cubists' pictorial innovations. Still, when Salvador Dalí's *Persistence of Memory*, 1931 (fig. 29), is compared with Gris's *Guitar and Music Paper* (cat. 80) of only six years earlier, an understanding of this period and its shared aspirations emerges.

"Cubism was simply a new way of representing the world," Gris wrote.[148] Having subscribed to the most utterly modern language, Gris turned it to use in producing an heir of history. The Louvre and the Prado were the backdrops of his fondest dreams; most fecund was the tradition of still life for attaining absolute statements. That tradition provided the conventions of microcosm to macrocosm transference, allegorical subjects, and an inherent mystery with regard to the object. Specifically, Gris followed still-life models having to do with the pure realm of art about art. Thus, that most sensitive of his admirers, Gertrude Stein, could write that for Gris "still life is a religion,"[149] and that he "combines perfection with transubstantiation."[150]

Fig. 29 Salvador Dalí
The Persistence of Memory, 1931
Oil on canvas
24.1 x 33 cm. (9½ x 13 in.)
The Museum of Modern Art, New York
Anonymous gift

Guitar and Music Paper, 1926–27 (cat. 80)

Notes

Complete information for shortened references in the footnotes may be found in the bibliography. References to Gris, *Letters*, make use of the numbering system employed in that volume.

1 Gertrude Stein, "Pictures of Juan Gris," p. 46.

2 Juan Gris, "Réponse à l'enquête 'chez les cubistes,'" reprinted in English in Daniel-Henry Kahnweiler, *Juan Gris: His Life and Work*, p. 145 (hereafter referred to as Kahnweiler).

3 Amédée Ozenfant, *Foundations of Modern Art*, p. 104.

4 Juan Gris, Untitled biography of Juan Gris [signed "Vauvrecy"], Kahnweiler, p. 138.

5 Juan Gris, "Des possibilités de la peinture," Kahnweiler, p. 140; idem, *Letters of Juan Gris*, LXXXIX.

6 Charles Sterling, *Still Life Painting* (New York and Paris: Universe Press, 1959), pp. 68–72.

7 Gertrude Stein, *Picasso*, p. 13.

8 Gris, *Letters*, CXLVI.

9 Gris, "Possibilités," p. 140.

10 Ibid., p. 143.

11 Amédée Ozenfant, *Mémoires*, p. 132.

12 See n. 139.

13 Maurice Raynal, "Juan Gris et la métaphore plastique," pp. 63–65.

14 John Golding, *Cubism: A History and an Analysis 1907–1914*, p. 96.

15 Gris, *Letters*, XCII.

16 Kahnweiler, p. 59.

17 José Chocano, *Alma América*, p. 51.

18 Douglas Cooper, *Juan Gris: Catalogue raisonné de l'oeuvre peint*, p. XIII (hereafter referred to as Cooper, *Catalogue*).

19 Juan Antonio Gaya-Nuño, *Juan Gris*, p. 52.

20 Kahnweiler, p. 6.

21 Gris, *Letters*, XCII.

22 See Kahnweiler's description of life at rue Ravignan, pp. 3–36.

23 Ibid., p. 4.

24 Gino Severini, *Tutta la vita di un pittore*, p. 90.

25 Cf. Léger, *The Smokers*, 1911–12, The Solomon R. Guggenheim Museum, New York.

26 See Cooper, *Catalogue*, nos. 4–5.

27 Guillaume Apollinaire, *Les peintres cubistes*, p. 61.

28 Lynn Gamwell, *Cubist Criticism*, p. 38.

29 It has been suggested that Balla was an influence on Gris at this time (James Thrall Soby, *Juan Gris*, p. 20).

30 Maurice Raynal, "L'exposition de 'La section d'or,'" p. 5; quoted in Edward Fry, *Cubism*, p. 100.

31 *The Washstand*, 1912 (Cooper, *Catalogue*, no. 26).

32 Apollinaire, p. 17; quoted in Fry, p. 116.

33 See Gris, *Letters*, CXXIV.

34 For more on Gris's use of the golden section, see William A. Camfield, "Juan Gris and the Golden Section," pp. 128–34.

35 I thank Ron Johnson for suggesting this line of comparison.

36 Kahnweiler, p. 83.

37 This comparison is also made by Robert Rosenblum, *Cubism and Twentieth-Century Art*, pp. 112, 121. The reproduction of the Cézanne in Rosenblum, p. 114, is cropped on all sides except the top.

38 Raynal, "L'exposition," p. 5; quoted in Fry, p. 100.

39 Golding, p. 180.

40 Jean Cocteau, *Professional Secrets: An Autobiography of Jean Cocteau*, trans. Richard Howard (New York: Farrar, Straus & Giroux, 1970), p. 75.

41 Christopher Green, *Léger and the Avant-Garde*, pp. 268–75.

42 From André Salmon, "Testimony against Gertrude Stein," *Transition* (Paris, February 1935), p. 14; quoted in Fry, p. 69.

43 Gris, *Letters*, III.

44 Gris, "Possibilités," p. 144.

45 Maurice Raynal, "Juan Gris," 1925, p. 5.

46 Ron Johnson, "Picasso's Musical and Mallarméan Constructions," *Arts* 51 (1977): 124.

47 Kahnweiler, p. 26.

48 For a discussion of Braque's and Picasso's use of musical instruments, see Siegfried Gohr, "Figur und Stilleben in der kubistischen Malerei von Picasso und Braque," *Kubismus* (Cologne: Josef-Haubrich-Kunsthalle, 1982), pp. 110–14; Johannes Langner, "Figur und Saiteninstrument bei Picasso," *Pantheon* 40 (1982): 98–113.

49 Gris, *Letters*, XCIII.

50 Christopher Gray, *Cubist Aesthetic Theories*, p. 98.

51 Picasso was probably the first, in 1912, to cover the canvas with pasted paper; see, for example, Pierre Daix, Joan Rosselet, *Picasso: The Cubist Years 1907–1914*, trans. S. Blair (Boston: New York Graphic Society, 1979), no. 513. Chris Poggi has kindly informed me that Boccioni's *Still Life* at the Yale University Art Gallery is covered with paper fragments and dated 1912. Given Picasso's and Braque's evolution of *papier collé*, the date of the Boccioni would appear to be unlikely.

52 Golding, p. 106.

53 Clement Greenberg, *Art and Culture* (Boston: Beacon Press, 1961), p. 81.

54 For more on Gris's use of headlines, see Robert Rosenblum, "Picasso and the Typography of Cubism," pp. 40–41.

55 Ibid., pp. 34–40.

56 Cooper, *Catalogue*, no. 73.

57 Ibid., no. 70.

58 Ibid., no. 87.

59 Gris, *Letters*, XXXI.

60 Ibid.

61 Cooper, *Catalogue*, nos. 140–43.

62 Gris, *Letters*, XXXV.

63 For Gris's influence on Matisse, see Kahnweiler, 11; Alfred H. Barr, Jr., *Matisse: His Art and Public* (New York: Museum of Modern Art, 1951), p. 168; Lisa Lyons, "Matisse: Work, 1914–1917," pp. 74–75. One is tempted to suggest that Matisse's use of black during the war owes its application to a growing familiarity with Gris's art. Moreover, subsequent to their meeting, Matisse showed a Gris-like interest in old master still-life painting, creating his *Variation of a Still Life by Jan Davidsz de Heem*, 1915 (Marx Collection). Then, in *Violinist at the Window*, 1917–18 (Musée Nationale d'Art Moderne Paris), Matisse anticipated the Grisean iconography of 1921 in which a musical instrument appears before the open window.

64 For more discussion of this subject, see Carla Gottlieb, *The Window in Art: From the Window of God to the Vanity of Man* (New York: Abaris, 1981). Delaunay's use of the window is also part of the context with which Gris would have been familiar.

65 Lorenz Eitner, "Open Window and the Storm-Tossed Boat: An Essay in the Iconography of Romanticism," *Art Bulletin* 37 (1955): 285.

66 Douglas Cooper, *The Cubist Epoch*, pp. 223–24.

67 Christopher Green, "Synthesis and the 'Synthetic Process' in the Painting of Juan Gris 1915–19," p. 90.

68 E. A. Carmean, Jr., "Juan Gris' 'Fantômas,'" p. 118.

69 Kahnweiler, p. 90; Green calls this an "object idea" ("Synthesis," p. 89).

70 Pierre Reverdy, *Au soleil du plafond* (Paris: Paul Birault, 1980). For the history of this collaboration, see pp. 157–60.

71 Ibid., p. 7; "Sur la nappe il y avait quelques grains de poudre ou de café. La guerre ou le repos sur les fronts qui se rident ensemble. L'odeur mêlée aux cris du soir, tout le monde ferme les yeux et le moulin broyait du noir comme nos têtes. Dans le cercle des voix, un nuage s'élève. Une vitre à la lèvre qui brouille nos pensées."

72 Kahnweiler, p. 26.

73 G. Cook, *Mallarmé: Selected Prose Poems, Essays and Letters* (Baltimore: Johns Hopkins University Press, 1956), p. 83.

74 Johnson, pp. 122–27.

75 Discussed in Reverdy, *Soleil*, p. 159.

76 See "Anguish of Fate" in Pierre Reverdy, *Reverdy*, trans. Anne Hyde Greet (Santa Barbara: Unicorn Press, 1968), p. 17.

77 For example, "Path," ibid., p. 15.

78 Reverdy, *Soleil*, p. 10: "L'ombre, le musicien, l'immense rideau bleu qui partage l'espace. C'est son nom qui frappe le battant, c'est l'air qui glisse mieux. Assis sur le versant profond d'une colline, entre les murs en creux, j'entends courir les signes plus vite que mes yeux. Entre les murs, devant le ciel, la fenêtre au milieu, les pieds sur le tapis où s'éteignent les étincelles, ou les étoiles, ou quelques autres signes lumineux."

79 "Le Livre," ibid., p. 11: "Contre le mur, l'auteur inquiet qui regarde vivre le monde et ne suit pas."

80 "Figure," ibid., p. 8; "Le Livre," ibid., p. 11; "Musicien," ibid., p. 10.

81 "Entre les 4 murs et sur la table." This passage was initially envisioned as the title for *Soleil* (ibid., p. 163).

82 Gris, *Letters*, XL.

83 Cooper, *Epoch*, p. 224.

84 Gris had begun using pointillist effects as early as 1914, e.g., Cooper, *Catalogue*, no. 112.

85 Gris, *Letters*, LII.

86 Ibid., LXII.

87 Sterling, p. 69.

88 Ibid., p. 70.

89 Pierre Reverdy, *Le gant de crin* (Paris: Libraire Plon, 1926), pp. 31–32.

90 Ozenfant, *Mémoires*, p. 91.

91 Cf. Lipchitz's work at this time (Cooper, *Epoch*, p. 228).

92 Green, *Léger*, pp. 273–74.

93 Kahnweiler, p. 104.

94 Green, "Synthesis," pp. 92–93.

95 Green, *Léger*, pp. 130–32.

96 For example, see Gris, *Letters*, LXXX, CXXIV.

97 Ibid., LVIII, LIX, LXI, LXXIII.

98 Ibid., LXXX.

99 Cocteau, pp. 74–75.

100 Jean Cocteau, *Five Days* (New York: Hill and Wang, 1961), pp. 2–3.

101 Pierre Reverdy, *Selected Poems*, trans. Kenneth Rexroth (New York: New Directions, 1955), p. viii.

102 Cocteau, *Autiobiography*, p. 75.

103 Greenberg, p. 82.

104 Ibid., p. 87.

105 Gris, *Letters*, CXXIV.

106 Lipchitz said Gris revered the triangle (Soby, p. 57).

107 Meyer Schapiro, *Modern Art: 19th & 20th Centuries* (New York: George Braziller, 1978), pp. 20–21.

108 Edward Fry, "Léger and the French Tradition," *Fernand Léger* (New York: Abbeville Press, 1982), p. 20.

109 Léger made use of a similar "spirit" in the following year, in *Man in the City*, 1919 (The Peggy Guggenheim Collection, Venice).

110 Gris, *Letters*, LXXII.

111 Ibid., CIII.

112 Gottlieb, pp. 285–86.

113 Ibid.

114 Ibid., p. 206.

115 Mark Rosenthal, "The Prototypical Triangle of Paul Klee," *Art Bulletin* 64 (1982): 299–310.

116 Ibid., pp. 300–301.

117 William Rubin, ed., *Pablo Picasso: A Retrospective Exhibition* (New York: Museum of Modern Art, 1980), p. 224.

118 Kahnweiler, p. 9.

119 Ozenfant, *Mémoires*, p. 91; Kahnweiler, p. 11.

120 Gris, "Notes sur ma peinture," Kahnweiler, p. 138.

121 Gris, "Possibilités," p. 141.

122 Dr. Philip Sandblom, in Abel Ulf, ed., *The Grace and Philip Sandblom Collection*, pp. 162–64.

123 Gris, *Letters*, CCXLV.

124 Cooper, *Catalogue*, no. 548.

125 Ibid., no. 512.

126 Gris, *Letters*, CCXII, CCXIII.

127 Stéphane Mallarmé, *Poems*, trans. Roger Fry (New York: New Directions, 1951), p. 91.

128 For a fuller discussion of Gris's health problems, see Sandblom, pp. 162–64.

129 See Lipchitz's comments, Soby, p. 73.

130 Cooper, *Epoch*, p. 197.

131 Gertrude Stein, *The Autiobiography of Alice B. Toklas*, p. 260

132 Gertrude Stein, "The Life of Juan Gris," p. 49.

133 Stein, *Autiobiography*, p. 260.

134 Ibid., p. 111.

135 Ibid., p. 259.

136 Ibid., p. 260.

137 Maurice Raynal, *Juan Gris*; see Exhibition Catalogues, Galerie Simon, 1923, [1]. The translation was kindly provided by Meg Grasselli.

138 From Maurice Raynal, *Quelques intentions du cubisme* (Paris, 1919); quoted in Fry, p. 152.

139 For indications of Gris's preference for Raynal and his theories, especially as opposed to Reverdy's, see Gris, Untitled biography, p. 138; Gris, *Letters*, LVIII, LIX, LXI, LXXIII, LXXXIX. In an unpublished conversation with Elise Goldstein (September 11, 1982), the artist's son Georges Gonzalez-Gris, reported that Raynal was the critic Gris preferred to all others.

140 Discussed by Gamwell, p. 47. See also Raynal, *Quelques intentions*. Gris wrote that he was seeking a "primary idea . . . of the object which is human and common to everyone" ("Possibilitiés," p. 140), then "one can say that . . . the aesthetic is the sum of the relationships between the painter and the outside world, relationships which culminate in the choice of subject" (ibid., p. 141). He wrote of the need to determine the subject in order to prevent the viewer from doing so (ibid., p. 142). "Artists of considerable stature have sometimes lacked style owing to a bad choice of subject" (ibid., p. 143). The "only purpose of any picture is to achieve representation" (ibid., p. 144).

141 Kahnweiler, p. 70.

142 Gris spoke of "an imaginary reality" ("Notes," p. 138; *Letters*, LXXX). Max Jacob wrote of making "the illusion real" (quoted in Kahnweiler, p. 126). Reverdy, too, sought a "poetic reality" (*Gant*, p. 16). Cocteau transferred the concept to the stage, writing of the "poetry of the theater" (*Five Plays*, p. 2).

143 Ozenfant defined the "Cubist attitude" as "the effort to evoke emotion" (*Foundations*, p. 55). Raynal discussed Gris's "émotion" in "Juan Gris," 1925, p. 5.

144 For a discussion of the metaphor, see Raynal, "Métaphore," pp. 63–65. See Kahnweiler, p. 128, and Ozenfant, *Mémoires*, p. 132.

145 Gris, Untitled biography, p. 138.

146 Gris, Untitled statement on Negro art, p. 137; also Untitled biography, p. 138.

147 Gris, *Letters*, CXXIV.

148 Gris, "Réponse," p. 144.

149 Stein, *Picasso*, p. 13.

150 Stein, "Pictures," p. 46.

Juan Gris, 1922
Photo: Man Ray
Yale Collection of American Literature
The Beinecke Rare Book and Manuscript Library

Chronology

The published works of Douglas Cooper and the late Daniel-Henry Kahnweiler have been the most valuable sources for this chronology. That material has been augmented through interviews kindly granted to the author in September 1982 by M. Georges Gonzalez-Gris, Mme Louise Leiris, and M. Maurice Jardot. In addition, Mme Josette Gris graciously provided information through Mme Leiris.

1887

March 23. José Victoriano Carmelo Carlos González Pérez, who will later call himself Juan Gris, is born at 4, Calle del Carmen, Madrid. Parents are Isabella Pérez Brasategui, age thirty-six, a native of Málaga, Andalusia, in southern Spain, and Gregorio González y Rodríguez, age forty-four, a native of Valladolid, Old Castile, in northwestern Spain. He is the thirteenth of fourteen children, only four of whom survive to adulthood. Though Gregorio is a successful merchant at the time of his son's birth, his business declines during the next several years, and the family is forced to relocate several times during Gris's childhood.

1902

Gris enters Escuela de Artes y Manufacturas (later known as Escuela Industrial), Madrid. Studies mathematics, physics, engineering, and scientific methods. Has drawings included in prominent illustrated journals *Blanco y Negro* and *Madrid Cómico*, both published in the Spanish capital.

1904

Abandons studies at Escuela in order to study painting with academic landscape and genre painter José Moreno Carbonero in Madrid and devote full time to his art. (Carbonero is also instructor to Salvador Dalí in 1921.)

Friendships with Willy Geiger, the German painter, who is a frequent contributor to Art Nouveau journal *Jugend*; George Kars, the Czechoslovakian Impressionist painter; Daniel Vásquez Díaz, the Spanish painter; the writer Pedro Penzol, and probably Eulogio Varela, Art Nouveau caricaturist for *Blanco y Negro*.

Rents space in studio on the Calle de Martín de los Heros.

1906

Spring. Gris illustrates *Alma América, Poemas indoespañoles* by José Santos Chocano, a Peruvian poet. Signs one illustration "J. Gris," first known use of this pseudonym. (Signs himself occasionally as Victoriano González as late as 1911.)

May. Edition of *Blanco y Negro* includes illustrations by Gris for two sonnets by Chocano and, in September, the magazine publishes "La conquista del pan. Apuntas para una comedia modernista" (The conquest of bread. Notes for a modernistic comedy), a story by Spanish author Francisco Flores García, with three illustrations by Gris.

September. Influenced by Díaz, who has moved to Paris, Gris decides to emigrate. In 1947, Kahnweiler would write,

> To his sister Antonieta he confided the secret of his impending departure. They scraped together all the money they could between them, sold everything, including Gris's bed and mattress, and in the end had just enough to pay for his journey. "When he finally landed in Paris," she wrote, "he had just sixteen francs in his pocket." [Daniel-Henry Kahnweiler, *Juan Gris, His Life and Work*, p. 6]

Late September. Greeted by Díaz at the Orsay train station, Paris. Checks into Hôtel Caulincourt in Montmartre district, where Díaz also lives. Upon arrival, Gris does not speak French. By moving to France, he is able to avoid mandatory military service in his native land, but because he does not pay the exemption tax, Gris is legally considered "criminal" in Spain and is unable to return there.

Through Díaz, meets another Spanish expatriate, Pablo Picasso, in his studio in Montmartre at 13, rue Ravignan (now Place Emile Goudeau). The building is known as "Le Bateau Lavoir" (The Laundry Barge), a name bestowed by poet Max Jacob, who lives at 7, rue Ravignan. Gris and Picasso become good friends. Picasso, whom Gris will jokingly refer to as "maître," finds studio and living space for Gris in basement of Bateau Lavoir.

Picasso executes preliminary studies for his painting *Les demoiselles d'Avignon.*

Gris also meets and becomes friends with writers Guillaume Apollinaire, André Salmon, and Max Jacob. Becomes known as "Jean" to most friends.

Earns living by contributing illustrations to satirical Spanish magazines.

Fauves are dominant avant-garde group of artists in France.

October 22. Paul Cézanne dies at Aix-en-Provence, in the south of France. Ten of his paintings are exhibited at the Salon d'Automne, held in Paris.

1907

Through Picasso, Gris meets Georges Braque and critic Maurice Raynal, who is to become one of his closest lifelong friends.

Memorial retrospective exhibition for Cézanne is organized at Salon d'Automne; fifty-six works shown.

Díaz paints Gris's portrait.

Winter. Daniel-Henry Kahnweiler, young ex-banker from Germany, opens art gallery at 28, rue Vignon, in the exclusive 9th district. Purchases paintings by André Derain, Maurice Vlaminck, Kees van Dongen, and Georges Braque, whose works he had seen at the Salon des Indépendants in March. Kahnweiler meets Braque, and also makes Picasso's acquaintance at Bateau Lavoir where he goes to view the artist's newly completed *Les demoiselles d'Avignon*, the painting that marks the debut of Cubism.

October or November. Picasso signs contract with Kahnweiler and meets Braque through Apollinaire.

November. First satirical drawing by Gris to be published in Paris appears in journal *Le Rire*. (Will submit work to this magazine until October 1911.)

1908

Kahnweiler shows paintings by Braque that were rejected at the Salon d'Automne. Hereafter, Kahnweiler will show continually changing sample of works by the artists, rather than solo exhibitions.

Gris meets Kahnweiler at Bateau Lavoir. Kahnweiler recalls first seeing Gris working there during his initial visits in 1907 to Picasso and, later, to Max Jacob:

> He was very young and, I thought, handsome, with dark brown hair and an olive complexion. He was more than just "the Spanish type"; he was a real example of what is commonly called "the creole type," that is to say he had almost a mulatto appearance. What struck one about his face were his very large brown eyes, the whites of which were bluish. It was Picasso who told me that his name was Juan Gris. . . . I learnt that Gris was starting to paint and often used to call on him as I went past. [Kahnweiler, p. 4]

Has drawings published in Parisian journals *Le Témoin, Cri de Paris, Le Charivari, L'Assiette au Beurre* (August 1908-August 1911), and in Barcelona, *Papitú* (December 1908-July 1912).

1909

At Bateau Lavoir, Gris moves into larger space with windows facing Place Ravignan; studio had previously been occupied by van Dongen.

April 9. Lucie Belin, Gris's young French mistress, gives birth to their son, Georges. While there is no documentation as to how long Belin lived with Gris prior to Georges's birth, it is certain that they are together for several years during his infancy. When they separate, Georges is sent to Madrid to live with his father's brother and sister.

February 20. The Parisian daily newspaper *Le Figaro* publishes the first "Futurist Manifesto" by Filippo Marinetti, the Italian poet and novelist.

May 25. Louis Vauxcelles, in *Gil Blas*, comments on "bizarreries cubiques" in Braque's paintings shown at Salon des Indépendants.

Fall. Picasso moves out of Bateau Lavoir.

1910

Gris begins to paint, primarily naturalistic watercolors. Earliest known extant oil, and the only one to survive from this year, is *Siphon and Bottles* (cat. 1), which he will always display affixed to his studio wall.

Spring. Cubists represented at the Salon des Indépendants; Picasso and Braque refuse to participate.

Fall. Similar representation of Cubists at Salon d'Automne.

Through Max Jacob, Gris meets Pierre Reverdy, who has recently come to Paris and moved to rue Ravignan near Bateau Lavoir. Gris will introduce him to Picasso, Braque, Raynal, and others.

1911

Gris's style rapidly assumes Cubist orientation. Paints his earliest portraits, of Raynal and Señor Legua.

First sale of paintings, among them, *The Book* (cat. 2) and *Bottle and Pitcher* (cat. 3), to Clovis Sagot, a contact made through Picasso. Sagot's gallery is near

Portrait of Daniel-Henry Kahnweiler, 1921 (cat. 97)

that of Ambroise Vollard in Montmartre.

Has drawings published in satirical magazines *L'Esquella de la Torratxa* (through 1914) and *La Campagna de Gracia* in Barcelona.

Spring. At Salon des Indépendants, Cubists are once more represented; Picasso and Braque are again absent.

Fall. Salon d'Automne occurs without their participation.

1912

January. Gris has first exhibition (fifteen works) at Sagot's gallery.

January-February. Work is discussed by Salmon in *Paris-Journal* (January 21) and Apollinaire in *Mercure de France* (February 16).

Paints Picasso's portrait and titles it *Homage to Picasso*.

Spring. According to Kahnweiler, *Homage* is one of three paintings included in Cubist section of Salon des Indépendants. Reviewed by Salmon, Apollinaire, and Raynal, among others. Apollinaire's article, in *L'Intransigeant*, March 25, includes the following passage about Gris: "Juan Gris is exhibiting an *Homage to Picasso* that reveals a praiseworthy effort and a noble disinterestedness. Juan Gris's exhibit could be entitled 'Integral Cubism.'"

April 1. Reverdy rents space at Bateau Lavoir, opposite that of Gris; remains through February 1913. Gris exhibits five paintings and three drawings in group show of Cubists at Galerias Dalmau, Barcelona, April 20-May 10. This is first time his paintings are shown in Spain. Article published in Barcelona's *La Publicidad* (author is probably José Junoy) mentioning Gris's "special deductive structure and geometrical conformation" is first review to focus on Gris alone.

Summer. Two paintings selected for inclusion in Cubist exhibition of Société de Peinture de Rouen, June 15-July 15.

Article by La Brosse titled "Silhouettes: Juan Gris," published in July 22 issue of *Paris-Journal*, is first commentary in French publication devoted to him.

Formulates "grid" system of composition which has impact on French artists Albert Gleizes, Jean Metzinger, and Louis Marcoussis.

September. Uses *papier collé* (pasted paper) for first time in *The Watch* (cat. 11), following use of collage earlier in the year by Picasso and Braque.

Participates in *La section d'or* (The Golden Section) exhibition, with paintings *Houses in Paris* (cat. 4) and *Man in the Café* (cat. 10), along with collages *The Washstand* (then titled *The Hairdresser*) and *The Watch* (cat. 11). *The Hairdresser*, onto which are affixed pieces of glass, is denounced by several baffled critics yet supported by Apollinaire. In Apollinaire's article in *L'Intransigeant* (October 10), Gris is dubbed "demon of logic." Exhibition held at Galerie La Boétie (October 10–30) marks second undertaking of the *Section d'or* or Puteaux group (their nickname: a reference to suburb of Paris where some of its adherents reside) headed by the Duchamp brothers, Gleizes, Metzinger, Fernand Léger, Alexander Archipenko, and Gris.

Agrees to contract with Kahnweiler, who intends to purchase and control exhibition of all future work. Years later, following Gris's premature death, Gertrude Stein will write of Kahnweiler's importance to Gris, "No one can say that Henry Kahnweiler can be left out of him" (from "The Life and Death of Juan Gris"). Kahnweiler also negotiates similar terms with Braque, Picasso, Léger, and Spanish sculptor Manolo Hugué.

Herman Rupf, of Bern, purchases his first Gris painting through Kahnweiler. From then on, is a steady client of Gris's work.

Josette Herpin joins Gris at Bateau Lavoir.

Salmon, in *La jeune peinture française*, includes commentary on Gris:

> *A thinking painter, he is not, however, entirely dominated by logic alone. With him a very deep moral purity takes the place of imagination. He is the only one who, while remaining shut up in a tight circle of plastic conditions, all defined and chosen by himself, has conveyed year after year, the immediate feeling of an opening out through broadening.* [English translation in Juan Antonio Gaya-Nuño, *Juan Gris*, p. 261]

1913

In London, the Vorticist movement begins.

Summer. Gris and Josette spend early summer in Rousillon, not far from Lyons.

August. Move to Céret and are frequently visited by Picasso, Manolo Hugué, and Frank Haviland, an American painter who uses pseudonym Frank Burty. Gris meets Michael Brenner, who expresses interest in his work. Brenner, an American sculptor, with his friend R.J. Coady operates Washington Square Gallery in New York and exhibits works by Cubist painters and other French avant-garde artists.

September 17. Gris writes to Kahnweiler, "I am working hard and seem to see more clearly certain things which I could not manage in Paris" (Douglas Cooper, ed. and trans., *Letters of Juan Gris, 1913–1927*, III).

Publication of Apollinaire's *Les peintres cubistes: Méditations esthétiques.* In his chapter concerning Gris he writes,

> Here is the man who has meditated on everything modern, here is the painter who wants to conceive only new structures, whose aim is to draw or paint nothing but materially pure forms.
>
> . . . His painting . . . seems to aim, above all, at scientific reality. . . .
>
> This art, if it perseveres in the direction it has taken, may end, not with scientific abstraction, but with that aesthetic arrangement which, after all, is the highest goal of scientific art. [English translation, pp. 41–43]

The dealer Léonce Rosenberg and Gertrude Stein, who had moved to Paris in 1903 and whose residence serves as a meeting place for American and European artists and writers, purchase their first paintings by Gris.

November. Gris returns to Paris.

Once again not invited to participate in either Salon des Indépendants or Salon d'Automne; also absent from *The International Exhibition of Modern Art*, called the Armory Show, New York, although other Cubists exhibit.

1914

Gris does collages almost exclusively.

June 28. Gris and Josette depart for Collioure, fishing town near Céret and Spanish border in eastern Pyrenees; lodge at rue de l'Eglise.

World War I disperses adherents of Parisian Cubism. Braque, Apollinaire, Derain, Marcoussis, Léger, Salmon, Raynal, and Jacques Vaillant (painter who lives at Bateau Lavoir), among others, enter military service.

July. Kahnweiler, subject to persecution because of his German citizenship, leaves Paris with wife, Lucie. Travel first to Rome and Siena, then establish residence in Bern for duration of war. Kahnweiler first sends Gris money but cannot sustain support for more than several months. This results in a temporary cessation of business relations between them.

Summer. Picasso at Avignon. He and Gris correspond.

Braque is in Sorgues and is called to service from there.

September. Gris forms close friendships with French artists Albert Marquet and Henri Matisse.

October. Stein, having learned of Gris's financial straits, sends him 200 francs. Matisse sees her in Paris and arranges that she and Brenner provide Gris with 125 francs monthly in exchange for pictures. Brenner proposes to borrow some of Gris's work and exhibit it in New York.

October 30. Gris's concern about friends is expressed in letter to Kahnweiler:

> Matisse also writes from Paris that: he has seen Mme. Derain, who is rather hard up, and Derain is in the front line; that Vlaminck is painting for the army at Le Havre, and that Picasso, from whom I have heard nothing for two months although I have written to him, withdrew a large sum—they say one hundred thousand francs—from a bank in Paris on the outbreak of war. People are surprised that he sent me 20 frs. Gleizes wounded. Segonzac also. De la Fresnaye, who volunteered, is sick at base camp. I have no news of Braque, the one person who interests me most.
> [*Letters*, XIX]

November. Gris outlines the terms of Brenner's proposal for Kahnweiler, who promptly informs Gris that he doubts he has the right to approve project under current political situation and considers such dealings as violations of their contract. Gris protests this response, but then

Amedeo Modigliani
Juan Gris, ca. 1915
Oil on canvas
54.9 x 38.1 cm. (21⅝ x 15 in.)
The Metropolitan Museum of Art
Bequest of Miss Adelaide Milton de Groot, 1967

concedes. No pictures are forwarded to Brenner and Stein; the misunderstanding leads to an abrupt break in relations between Gris and his two benefactors.

December 20. Beginning of copious correspondence with Raynal. In first letter, he writes,

> Don't get discouraged or pessimistic. You'll come back; we are still young and there is certainly a rosy future ahead of us. Only for some is the war a misfortune, for others it is a break in the day-to-day struggle which they have been engaged in for years. My present life is flat, undecided and sterile and I don't even like reading the newspapers because I am so impressed and terrified by what is happening. Obviously I have no self-control. My only wish is that it should end soon and that my friends return. [Letters, XXV]

1915

January. Rosenberg attempts to convince Gris to sell him paintings directly; Gris refuses because of existing contract with Kahnweiler.

March 26. Gris writes optimistically of his recent work in letter to Kahnweiler:

> I think I have really made progress recently and that my pictures begin to have a unity which they have lacked until now. They are no longer those inventories of objects which used to depress me so much. But I still have to make an enormous effort to achieve what I have in mind. For I realize that although my ideas are well enough developed, my means of expressing them plastically are not. In short, I have not got an aesthetic, and this I can only acquire by experience. [Letters, XXXI]

April. By common agreement, terms of contract are suspended between Gris and Kahnweiler.

April 19. Gris describes situation in Paris to Kahnweiler:

> You who are absent cannot imagine how every foreigner here is suspect, no matter what his nationality may be. . . . I think it is much better for us to carry on our correspondence via Madrid in order not to arouse my concierge's suspicions. I can see you laughing at my suggestion. But don't forget that at the present time nothing is more important than the opinion and the respect of a concierge. . . . They say appalling things in the canteens of Montmartre and make terrible accusations against myself and against everyone who has had dealings with you. So I have not been able to go and eat in them . . . life at this moment is not much fun and although I used to be very fond of Paris I would gladly leave it now. [Letters, XXXII]

Summer. Sees Metzinger often.

Illustrates with several drawings Reverdy's *Poèmes en prose;* published by Paul Birault, October 12.

June. Does first "open window" painting, *Still Life and Landscape—Place Ravignan,* incorporating indoor and outdoor views.

June 1. Gris writes to Kahnweiler,

> You asked about Braque. . . . Yesterday he was brought to a hospital here. I expect to see him tomorrow. . . . We knew that he had been wounded, but for a whole fortnight we did not know just what had happened. . . . He's a wonderful person. I have been terribly worried on his account, because as you know, I am very fond of him. [Letters, XXXV]

Adolphe Basler, dealer and critic, visits Gris often.

December 15. Apparently a temporary and unforeseen break in steady correspondence between Kahnweiler and Gris for remainder of war. In last letter for the period, Gris writes,

> Sometimes I feel that my way of painting is wholly mistaken. I can't find room in my pictures for that sensitive and sensuous side which I feel should always be there. Perhaps I make the mistake of looking for the pictorial qualities of an earlier artform in one which is new. . . . I find my pictures excessively cold. But Ingres too is cold, and yet he is good. Seurat also . . . although I dislike the meticulous element in his pictures almost as much as in my own. Oh, how I wish I could convey the ease and the charm of the unfinished! [Letters, XL]

Amédée Ozenfant begins to publish *L'Elan*, a journal with a strong Cubist bias.

About this time, Amedeo Modigliani paints Gris's portrait.

Juan Gris at Beaulieu, 1916
Photo: Josette Gris

1916
Battle of Verdun, the longest and costliest battle of the war, is fought in northwestern France; nearly one million lives are lost.

Dada movement proclaims itself in Zurich.

Gris and Reverdy are commissioned by Léonce Rosenberg to collaborate on a book. (The twenty prose poems are ultimately published by Tériade with eleven lithographs by Gris.)

Summer. Gris goes with Josette to Beaulieu near Loches, in her native region of Touraine, west central France.

Friendship with André Level, proprietor of Galerie Percier in Paris. In *Souvenirs d'un collectioneur*, Level mentions accompanying Léonce Rosenberg to Gris's studio during the war; later purchases paintings.

December 31. Gris helps to organize banquet to honor Apollinaire's release from hospital (where he was recovering from war wounds) and publication of his *Le poète assassiné*.

1917
January 15. Attends banquet in Paris held to celebrate Braque's recovery from war wound. Braque begins to paint again. Gris resumes close friendship with him for a time and also pursues friendship with sculptor Jacques Lipchitz.

Spring. Publication begins of *Nord-Sud*, literary and art review named after Paris subway line running from Montmartre to Montparnasse; edited by Pierre Reverdy, appears monthly for next two years.

April 6. United States declares war on Germany and enters combat.

May 18. Russian ballet performs *Parade* for first time at Théâtre du Châtelet, Paris. Scenario by Jean Cocteau, music by Erik Satie, decor by Picasso.

November. Gris makes polychrome plaster sculpture titled *Harlequin* (fig. 14).

Signs three-year contract with Rosenberg, with option to renew agreement for another three years. Rosenberg buys entire oeuvre from 1915 on.

1918
April. Gris and Josette return to Beaulieu. Visited by Lipchitz, Metzinger, Maria Blanchard (painter who studied in Madrid and then settled in Paris), and Vicente Huidobro (Chilean poet).

Rosenberg opens Galerie de l'Effort Moderne at 19, rue de la Beaume, in the Latin Quarter. In addition to Gris, represents Braque, Léger, Picasso, Gleizes, Laurens, and Lipchitz.

June 4. Gris writes from Beaulieu to Paul Dermée, "With the present sky, every day adds a grey hair and even my palette has become earthy" (*Letters*, LXVIII).

November. Gris returns to Paris.

November 9. Apollinaire dies of war injuries from 1916.

November 11. Armistice between Germany and the Allies signals a conclusion to World War I.

November 15. Ozenfant and Charles Jeanneret, who uses Le Corbusier as architectural pseudonym, publish *Après le cubisme* to coincide with exhibition of Purist painting they organize at Galerie Thomas, Paris.

December. Gris's drawings reproduced in third issue of *Dada*, periodical published by the movement in Zurich.

Dermée's *Beautés de 1918* published with cover and three drawings by Gris.

1919
Jeanneret and Ozenfant publish the review *L'Esprit Nouveau* in Paris and start Purist movement.

Reverdy's *La guitare endormie* published with four Gris drawings, including frontispiece portrait.

Valori Plastici, art review in Rome run by Mario Broglio, publishes statements by Gris in volume dedicated to Cubism:

> *Artists have thought to produce a poetic effect with beautiful models or beautiful subjects. We, on the other hand, believe that we can produce it with beautiful elements; for, those of the intellect are certainly the most beautiful.* [Kahnweiler, p. 137]

April. First retrospective exhibition of about fifty paintings from 1916–18 at Galerie de l'Effort Moderne. Rosenberg organizes literary gathering during exhibition and arranges to have Jean

Juan Gris at Place Ravignan in Montmartre, Paris, 1917
Photo: Josette Gris

Juan Gris and Josette Gris (left) with M. and Mme
Vicente Huidobro (center), their children, and M. and
Mme Jacques Lipchitz (right) at Beaulieu, 1918

Cocteau deliver address. This upsets Gris
who writes to Raynal on February 2,
"I was really cross about this because I
would have offered it to you, and I told him
so. His reply was that Cocteau had kindly
proposed himself and that he had not been
able to refuse" (*Letters*, LXXVI). Gris
objects to notion that Cocteau speak
"about painting" in front of his pictures.
Ultimately, Rosenberg organizes session
with introduction by Raynal, poetry read
by Cocteau, and music by Georges Auric.

August. Kahnweiler and Gris apparently
resume correspondence. In response of
August 25 to Kahnweiler's initial letter, Gris
summarizes his situation vis-à-vis his
contemporaries:

> *My exhibition took place in April last
> and had a certain amount of success.
> There were about fifty pictures painted
> in 1916, 17, and 18. They looked
> rather well as a group and a lot of
> people came. Yet I don't really know
> how much they liked it, for there is
> so much admiration for the sheerest
> mediocrity; people get quite excited
> about displays of chaos, but no one
> likes discipline and clarity. The exag-
> gerations of the Dada movement and
> others like Picabia make us look
> classical, though I can't say I mind
> about that. I would like to continue the
> tradition of painting with plastic
> means while bringing to it a new
> aesthetic based on the intellect. I think
> one can quite well take over Chardin's
> means without taking over either the
> appearance of his pictures or his
> conception of reality. Those who
> believe in abstract painting seem to
> me like weavers who think they can
> produce a material with threads
> running in one direction only and
> nothing to hold them together. When
> you have no plastic intention how
> can you control and make sense of
> your representational liberties? And
> when you are not concerned with
> reality how can you control and make
> sense of your plastic liberties?
>
> *For some time I have been rather
> pleased with my own work because I
> think that at last I am entering on
> a period of realization. . . . I have also
> managed to rid my painting of a too*

*brutal and descriptive reality. It has,
so to speak, become more poetic. I
hope that ultimately I shall be able to
express very precisely, and by means
of pure intellectual elements, an
imaginary reality. This really amounts
to a sort of painting which is inaccurate but precise, just the opposite
of bad painting which is accurate but
not precise. [Letters, LXXX]*

September. Kahnweiler notifies Gris of
wish to resume business association.
Asserts claim for pictures owed to him from
1914–15 under former contract; tries to
formulate new contract. Gris informs
Kahnweiler of exclusive contract he has had
with Rosenberg for past two years.

September 3. In letter to Kahnweiler,
Gris praises "the sudden crop of poets. . . .
Reverdy is one of the leaders and among
the best; he has had a great influence on
the young. . . . It is the Reverdy following
which has most kinship with our painting,
and they are breaking away more and
more from [Blaise] Cendrars and [Tristan]
Tzara." While discussing his own work,
Gris compliments Braque's new work but
informs Kahnweiler that he has felt slighted
by him:

*My work in its present stage can be
compared with those pictures of Seurat
in which the severity and the emptiness
are the result of inexperience and not
of incompetence. This is no longer
true of Braque, whose experience
begins to be considerable and now
enables him to bring off some magnificent pictures. (I am perhaps foolish to
say such nice things about him because
he has not behaved well towards me.)*

This is first of several indications of rift
between Gris and Braque during period
January 1917 to September 1919. There
is also a hint of coolness toward Picasso:

*Picasso produces fine things still when
he has the time between a Russian
ballet and a society portrait. [Letters,
LXXXI]*

October. Gris has saved works done
prior to 1915 for Kahnweiler; these twelve
sent to Kahnweiler while he is still in Bern.

1920

January. Spanish poet Guillermo de Torre
writes to Gris asking for statements on

his aesthetics. Gris responds on January 8:

*In spite of having many things to
say on the subject of art, I prefer to
express them solely in my painting
and never in writing. . . . I prefer to
use basic words in helping to make
clear certain spiritual characteristics
with respect to art generally and
painting in particular. . . .*

*. . . Your effort has all my sympathy,
and it is above all necessary in Spain,
where culture and the idea of art are
not very widespread. In any case,
as far as I know you are the first writer
in Spain to recognize that I exist.
[Letters, LXXXIX]*

Gris participates in last Cubist section
of the Salon des Indépendants.

January 31. Gris writes to Kahnweiler,
*The Salon des Indépendants has
opened with something of a success for
the Cubists who are taken seriously
by the whole—or almost—of the press.
Even M. Vauxcelles admits that he
has wronged us. . . . No one says much
about me because I'm a foreigner.
However several people have paid me
great compliments. Picasso has given
me a lot of support, and Gertrude
Stein, with whom I have not been on
good terms, told me that one of my
pictures was the best in the whole
Salon. On the other hand, Braque
refused to be hung in the same room
with me and is running me down
as much as he can. [Letters, XC]*

Gris's and Stein's differences reconciled.
In a letter of February 2, he responds to
her compliments about his paintings in the
Salon:

*I am greatly flattered by what you say
about my contribution to the Indépendants, more especially as I have a
great respect for your understanding of
painting. . . .*

*. . . I hope I shall have a chance
of seeing and talking to you. [Letters,
XCI]*

From this point on, Gris and Stein enjoy
a close friendship.

Gris tries to interest Kahnweiler in
Lipchitz's sculpture.

Has one-man show at Galerie Alfred
Flechtheim, Düsseldorf.

Kahnweiler returns to Paris from Bern.

Gris at Bandol, 1921
Josette Gris

April. Gris's statements "on Negro art" published in *Action:*

> Negro sculptures provide a striking proof of the possibilities of an anti-idealistic *art. Inspired by a religious spirit, they offer a varied and precise representation of great principles and universal ideas. How can one deny the name of art to a creative process which produces on this basis individualistic representations of universal ideas, each time in a different way? It is the reverse of Greek art, which started from the individual and attempted to suggest an ideal type.* [Kahnweiler, p. 137]

May. First term of contract with Rosenberg expires. Gris revises terms to allow himself option of contract with Kahnweiler, too. Each dealer to receive pictures of specified dimensions.

First symptoms of illness. Health worsens; condition diagnosed as pleurisy. Enters Tenon Hospital for treatment.

August 11. Discharged from hospital; takes train the following day to Beaulieu with Josette.

September. Resumes painting.

Kahnweiler opens Galerie Simon with partner André Simon, 29 bis, rue d'Astorg, Paris. Louise Godon, Kahnweiler's sister-in-law, becomes his assistant. (She will marry Michel Leiris, the poet, in 1927, and in 1941 will assume formal ownership of the gallery. At that time, Galerie Simon, being considered a Jewish business, is liquidated by governmental authorities; it is succeeded by Galerie Leiris, which Kahnweiler again directs after World War II.)

October. Gris returns to Paris with Josette. Visits Kahnweiler's new gallery.

Health still considered fragile; advised not to remain in Paris during winter.

November. Gris and Josette travel to Bandol-sur-Mer. Settle at 4, rue Nationale on November 30.

December. Works on commission for lithographs for *Ne coupez pas mademoiselle, ou les erreurs des P.T.T.* by Max Jacob. Published the following year.

Arrangement with both Kahnweiler and Rosenberg proves untenable, and Gris annuls agreement with the latter.

Raynal publishes *Juan Gris*.

Kahnweiler publishes *Der Weg zum Kubismus*, Munich.

Beginning of Picasso's Neoclassic period.

1921

January. Gris is distressed to learn that Kahnweiler's pre-war sequestered stock is to be sold at auction later in the year.

Instructs a pupil, the eleven-year-old son of his butcher, who assists with sketches of paintings during the first quarter of the year. Though sometimes impatient with the child, he does a lithograph portrait of him and is "upset" to see the family move away in March to the Cannes region.

February. Article on Gris with text by Raynal appears in *L'Esprit Nouveau*. Includes biography and notes on painting, which the article indicates have been compiled by Vauvrecy, the pseudonym of Ozenfant. Kahnweiler later indicates that they were written by Gris himself. On "his aesthetic," Gris writes,

> I work with the elements of the intellect, with the imagination. I try to make concrete that which is abstract. I proceed from the general to the particular, by which I mean that I start with an abstraction in order to arrive at a true fact. Mine is an art of synthesis, of deduction, as Raynal has said. . . .
>
> I consider that the architectural element in painting is mathematics, the abstract side; I want to humanize it. Cézanne turns a bottle into a cylinder, but I begin with a cylinder and create an individual of a special type: I make a bottle—a particular bottle—out of a cylinder. Cézanne tends toward architecture, I tend away from it. That is why I compose with abstractions (colours) and make my adjustments when these colours have assumed the form of objects.

Elsewhere in same essay he writes,

> Though in my system I may depart greatly from my any form of idealistic or naturalistic art, in practice I cannot break away from the Louvre. Mine is the method of all times, the method used by the old masters: there are technical means and they remain constant. [Kahnweiler, pp. 137–38.]

Emphasizes theme of the "open window" again.

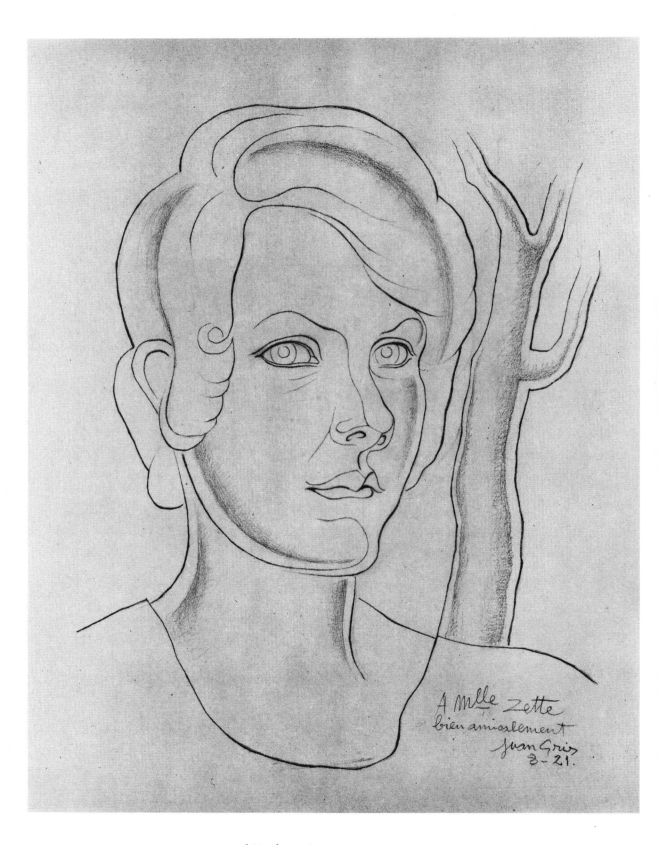

Portrait of Madame Louise Leiris, 1921 (cat. 98)

February 25. Dons Senegalese costume to attend Carnival dance and writes to Kahnweiler of it, "I have learnt to dance, more or less, and we go every Sunday night to the *Bal des Joyeux Bandolais*" (*Letters*, CXV).

Works on lithograph portraits (*Marcelle the Brunette, Marcelle the Blond, Jean the Musician* [Marcelle's brother], *The Child* [his pupil] and drawings.

February 26. In a letter to Raynal, Gris writes of his new pastime:

> I have learnt to dance and spend a lot of time doing it. I am also practising hypnotism on some remarkably good subjects whom I have found here.
> [*Letters*, CXVI]

March. Rosenberg exhibits early works by Gris at Galerie de l'Effort Moderne, March 1–25. Gris is not consulted in the organization of the exhibition and notes to Raynal and Kahnweiler that the situation worries him (*Letters*, CXVII).

Huidobro asks Gris to do a lithograph for a forthcoming book. *Tremblement de ciel* is published (n.d.) with Gris's portrait of the author.

March 25. In response to article by Ozenfant and Jeanneret, "Le Purisme," in the January issue of *L'Esprit Nouveau,* Gris writes to the former,

> You apparently reject the idea which I have on occasion put forward. . . . Remember that whereas a Greek artist took a particular Athenian woman and evolved an ideal and consequently generalised type of womanhood, the Church on the other hand took the abstract idea of God and turned it into gentle Jesus with his beard, moustache, cross and crown of thorns. Yes, I'm horribly Christian in that respect, because it's exactly my own procedure.
> [*Letters*, CXXIV]

April. Serge Diaghilev invites Gris to submit proposal for decor of *Cuadro flamenco,* suite of Andalusian dances and songs to music by Manuel de Falla. Gris goes to Monte Carlo from Bandol to discuss project.

April 14. Prior to departure, he is hesitant to accept the commission and writes to Kahnweiler,

> If I refuse I shall be flying in the face of fortune, since a ballet can help

> to make my name known and bring me admirers, whereas if I accept I shall be giving up my glorious tranquillity.
> [*Letters*, CXXVII]

Gris's reply telegram arrives at Monte Carlo past deadline Diaghilev had given. Gris arrives to find Diaghilev has changed plans and decided to engage Picasso, who has produced set of completed designs. Diaghilev implores Gris to remain for several days to do portraits of the two principal dancers; Gris concedes. These are included in the company program. In Monte Carlo for a week, he meets Mikhail Larionov and sees Matisse, Stein, and Alice Toklas.

Gris claims Stein is cross with Picasso for having usurped the commission, and she tells Gris she will assist him to secure another ballet commission (*Letters*, CXXX).

Gris returns to Bandol. Stein and Toklas visit for two days.

April 29. Writes of Monte Carlo to Raynal, "I was bored to death and found the place sinister to a degree. It's a sort of Universal Exhibition place, and the streets look terribly sad because they are smart" (*Letters*, CXXXI).

May–June. Josette undergoes series of operations on her right-hand thumb.

June. Gris considers leaving Josette to marry Marcelle, a wealthy young woman with whom he has fallen in love during the winter.

June 3–14. First sale of Kahnweiler's pre-war sequestered property held at Hôtel Drouot, Paris. Subsequent sales occur on November 17–18, 1921; July 4, 1922; May 7–8, 1922. Fifty-seven works by Gris sold at low prices compared to those paid for Picasso, Léger, André Derain, van Dongen, and others. Kahnweiler recovers portion of his stock.

June 22. Gris and Josette separate temporarily.

July. Gris returns to Paris.

October. Doctors counsel Gris not to remain in Paris for the winter. Reunited with Josette; they go to Céret.

Unable to find apartment, Gris and Josette establish residence at Hôtel Garretta.

November. See Manolo and wife daily. By the following month, Gris writes to Kahnweiler that Manolo "hates" his painting and they do not socialize.

Reads books about biology. Also particularly interested in Einstein's theories. Though feeling cut off from friends, intellectual discourse, etc., at Céret, Gris finds he is not depressed because of sense of accomplishment in work.

December. Valori Plastici considers doing monograph on Gris. In mid-December Gris write to Raynal that he wants to be classified as a French rather than Spanish contemporary painter in this book (*Letters*, CLII).

Joseph Brummer, an American collector, gives Gris's *Fruit Dish and Bottle*, 1916 (cat. 41), to Smith College, Northampton, making it the first painting by Gris to be placed in an American museum.

Kahnweiler begins to represent the sculptor Henri Laurens, about whom Gris had written to him in September 1919.

Juan Gris with Josette in his studio
at Le Bateau Lavoir, 1922
Photo: Daniel-Henry Kahnweiler

1922

January. Gris is angered that Gino Severini, the Italian artist who with Marinetti founded Futurism, has claimed in print that the deductive method was his own formulation. Writes to Raynal, "He [Severini] even cites my own example which appeared in the same number of E. N. [*L'Esprit Nouveau*] as your articles about me" (*Letters*, CLIV).

Spring. Gris and Josette return to Paris with improvement of weather. Move from studio at 13, rue Ravignan to three-room flat found for them by Mme Kahnweiler at 8, rue de la Mairie, Boulogne-sur-Seine, suburb of Paris. The dealer's family lives down the street at number 12 (now called rue de l'Ancienne Maire). Though move limits social activity, they see the Kahnweilers frequently. On Sundays invariably visited by a large group of friends, among them André Simon, the Raynals, Massons, Salacrous, Suzanne Roger and André Beaudin, Swiss writer Charles-Albert Cingria, painter Elie Lascaux, Antonin Artaud, writer Georges Limbour, Michel Leiris, Roland Tual, Erik Satie, Jacob, Tzara, poet/novelist Robert Desnos.

Stein sends good friend Kate Buss, journalist from Boston, to visit Gris in the hope that she will write article about him for Boston newspaper.

October. Gris hospitalized for operation of anal fistula; remains eight days.

November. Works on costumes and sets for Diaghilev production of eighteenth-century ballet *Les tentations de la bergère ou l'amour vanqueur* (The Temptations of the Shepherdess or Triumphant Love) with music by Montéclair, arranged by Henri Casadesus; choreography by Nijinska. Marks beginning of series of decors and costumes Gris will do for Diaghilev during year to come.

Man Ray makes a photographic portrait of Gris; later writes,

> *It was Gertrude Stein who insisted on my doing a portrait of Juan Gris. . . . whenever she loved someone, or made a new acquisition in a friend, he was brought to my studio to be photographed. . . . He [Gris] was the opposite of everything El Greco stands for. Very gentle yet strong, taciturn, brooding, like one who has accepted the haphazard injustices, indifferences and recognitions of this or any other world. He looked Spanish but there the resemblance stopped. I sat him against the wall with an American banjo hanging nearby. He liked that, I could see in his hard-rimmed eyes the project of a future painting forming itself. He had put on a high stiff collar for the occasion. . . .* [from *Picasso, Gris, Miró: The Spanish Masters of 20th-Century Painting*, see Exhibition Catalogues, San Francisco Museum of Art, p. 43]

1923

March. Gris requests that Stein come to view pictures of newly finished work before they are to be shown in solo exhibition at Galerie Simon, March 20–April 5.

Gris does small figures in painted sheet iron. Photographed and intended as illustrations for article by Tristan Tzara, one of founders of Dada, in *Vanity Fair*. (The article is never published.)

Der Querschnitt, Frankfurt am Main, edited by Alfred Flechtheim, publishes Gris's "Notes sur ma peinture" in summer volume:

> *. . . My technique is classical, for I have learnt it from the masters of the past.*
> *. . . My method of work is . . . deductive. It is not picture "X" which*

A dinner at the Huidobro's home in 1921–22. *Seated from left to right:* Lucie Kahnweiler, Juan Gris, Zdanevitch, Josette Gris, Fernand Léger, Daniel-Henry Kahnweiler, Jeanne Léger, Vicente Huidobro, Celine Arnauld (Mme Paul Dermée); *standing from left to right:* two unidentified guests, Paul Dermée, Waldemar George, Louise Godon (later, Mme Michel Leiris)

Maquette of the set for
Les tentations de la bergère, 1923

Maquette of the set for *La colombe*, 1923

manages to correspond with my subject, but subject "X" which manages to correspond with my picture.

I call this a deductive method because the pictorial relationships between the coloured forms suggest to me certain private relationships between the elements of an imaginary reality. The mathematics of picture-making lead me to the physics of representation. The quality or the dimensions of a form or a colour suggest to me the appellation or the adjective for an object. Hence, I never know in advance the appearance of the object represented. If I particularise pictorial relationships to the point of representing objects, it is in order that the spectator shall not do so for himself, and in order to prevent the combination of coloured forms suggesting to him a reality which I have not intended.

Now painting is foreseeing—foreseeing what will happen to the general effect of a picture by the introduction of some particular form or some particular colour, and foreseeing what sort of reality will be suggested to the spectator. . . .

I do not know if one can give to this aesthetic, this technique and this method, the name of Cubism. Anyway, I make no claim to represent any particular sort of appearance, be it Cubist or naturalistic. [Kahnweiler, p. 138]

June. Gris again collaborates with the Russian impresario on the Fête Merveilleuse held in Hall of Mirrors at Palace of Versailles.

October. Gris goes with Josette from Boulogne-sur-Seine to Beausoleil, near Monte Carlo, to work for Diaghilev.

Settles with Josette at Villa Tosca, 3, rue du Marché. Sees Stein and Matisse, who are residing in Nice, several times. Gris is bored for much of the time spent in midst of Diaghilev's company; only distraction is dancing at Café de Paris.

Diaghilev puts Gris to work on *La colombe* prior to completion of *Les tentations de la bergère.* . . . New project is an opera by Gounod for which Gris designs the decor.

December. Gris writes to Kahnweiler that he is anxious to leave Beausoleil, as he has difficulty combining painting and Diaghilev's projects:

I am very upset to hear your opinion of my pictures. Alas, you have merely confirmed my own fears. I was afraid of having taken a wrong turning. Thank you for having told me the truth, because you have stopped me going further in the wrong direction. Above all, don't hesitate to destroy them if you think they are not worthy of me. . . .

I really feel that I am going through a bad period. I don't feel confident with any medium and I'm utterly devoid of self-assurance in my work. [*Letters,* CLXXXVI]

Conceives decor and costumes for *L'éducation manquée* by Chabrier, which Picasso was to have done but cancelled at last moment.

December 31. In letter to Stein, Gris informs her that he has completed all work expected by Diaghilev: "I've had enough of the theatre. What a waste of time!" [*Letters,* CXCII]

1924

January. Premiere of three Diaghilev productions with decor and costumes by Gris.

Satie sides with Gris in his disgust with atmosphere in Monte Carlo; the composer has argued with Cocteau and Braque.

Gris and Josette return to Boulogne-sur-Seine, his health having suffered from climate in Beausoleil.

February. Gris begins work on illustrations for *Le casseur d'assiettes,* by Armand Salacrou. Four lithographs (one on the cover) appear in the book.

April. Gris invited by Dr. Allendy, who established Society of Philosphical and Scientific Studies, to deliver lecture at Sorbonne. Having prepared talk, "Des possibilités de la peinture," Gris has text critiqued by Stein.

May 15. Delivers the lecture. The text is translated into English and published in the June–July issue of *Transatlantic Review,* in Spanish in the September issue of *Alfar,* and in German in *Der Querschnitt* the following January:

In all great periods of art one senses

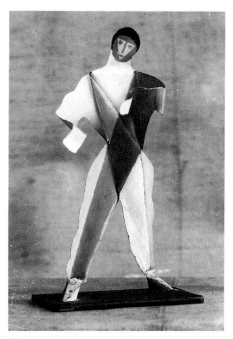

Pierrot, 1923
Painted metal
30 cm. high (11⅞ in.)
Private collection
(DC S. 6)

Juan Gris, 1924
Photo: Georges Duthuit

the desire to represent a substantial and spiritual world. The representation has been influenced and varied in accordance with the needs and obsessions of each age. The role of technique on each occasion has merely been to qualify this substantial world. Certain technical methods are common to all periods; others are less constant and vary according to the aesthetic. . . . Only the purely architectural element in painting has remained constant. . . . the only true pictorial technique is a sort of flat, coloured architecture. . . .

A picture with no representational purpose is to my mind always an incomplete technical exercise, for the only purpose of any picture is to achieve representation. Nor is a painting which is merely the faithful copy of an object a picture, for even supposing that it fulfills the conditions of coloured architecture, it still has no aesthetic, that is to say, no selection of the elements of the reality it expresses. It will only be the copy of an object and never a subject. . . .

. . . The essence of painting is the expression of certain relationships between the painter and the outside world, and that a picture is the intimate association of these relationships with the limited surface which contains them. [Kahnweiler, pp. 140–44]

May 28. Culmination of Gris's collaboration with Diaghilev: designs setting and costumes for Red Cross Festival at Parisian department store Grands Magasins du Printemps.

August. Jane Heap, editor of *The Little Review*, New York, meets Gris at the insistence of Stein, who wants Gris's work featured in future edition. Stein vows to write about the work herself. Gris is delighted with the idea.

August 17–23. Gris and Josette leave Boulogne-sur-Seine for brief vacation at Némours with André and Odette Masson, Armand and Lucienne Salacrou, Roland Tual, and Michel Leiris.

Autumn. The Little Review features eighteen reproductions of Gris's work accompanied by Stein's first article on Gris:

Juan Gris is a Spaniard. He says that his pictures remind him of the school Fontainbleau [sic]. The school of Fontainbleau is a nice school. Diana and others. In this he makes no mistake, but he never does make a mistake. He might and he is, he is and he might, he is right and he might be right, he is a perfect painter and he might be right. He is a perfect painter, alright, he might be right. [Autumn 1924–Winter 1925, p. 16]

December. Tristan Tzara asks Gris to illustrate publication of *Mouchoir de nuages* (published in 1925 with eight Gris etchings, one of which is on the cover).

In Paris, Breton publishes first Surrealist manifesto.

Gleizes publishes *La peinture et ses lois: ce qui devait sortir du cubisme.*

Léger produces his silent film *Ballet mécanique*, which is devoid of narrative content, communicating entirely by "objective imagery."

Tadeusz Peiper's *Żywe Linje* is published in Cracow with three drawings by Gris.

1925

January. Publication of article "Réponse à l'enquête 'chez les cubistes,'" in response to a questionnaire sent out by *Bulletin de la Vie Artistique*; contains text by Gris:

Cubism? As I never consciously, and after mature reflection, became a Cubist but, by dint of working along certain lines, have been classed as such, I have never thought about its causes and its character like someone outside the movement who has meditated on it before adopting it.

To-day I am clearly aware that, at the start, Cubism was simply a new way of representing the world.

. . . Cubism is not a manner but an aesthetic, and even a state of mind; it is therefore inevitably connected with every manifestation of contemporary thought. It is possible to invent a technique or a manner independently, but one cannot invent the whole complexity of a state of mind. [Kahnweiler, pp. 144–45]

Summer. Painting by Gris from Stein's collection is among modern pictures exhibited in the pavilion designed by Le Corbusier at *Exposition des arts décoratifs,*

Paris. Term "art deco" is derived from the exhibition. Gris visits it frequently.

August. Health declines. He and Josette, with Armand and Lucienne Salacrou, take short trip down the Seine estuary near Le Havre. While on vacation, Gris continues to work on illustrations for Tzara's book; one illustration selected for publication is portrait of captain of their boat.

August 18. Alphonse Kahn, well-known collector and dealer who resides at St. Germain-en-Laye, outskirts of Paris, visits and decides to purchase his first painting by Gris, the recently completed *The Blue Cloth* (cat. 75). Kahn's interest delights Gris, who had been distressed because the collector had previously purchased work by Picasso, Braque, and Léger, and had not acquired any of his. Kahn continues to acquire works by Gris.

November. First group exhibition of Surrealist painters at Galerie Pierre, Paris; includes Jean Arp, Giorgio de Chirico, Max Ernst, Paul Klee, André Masson, Joan Miró, Picasso, and Man Ray. In February 1926 Raynal and others are sent insulting letters by Surrealists; Gris takes offense and mentions it to Kahnweiler (see *Letters*, CCXVI).

November 20. Dr. G. F. Rever, collector from Lausanne, makes first purchase of Gris's work, buying twenty-eight pictures, fourteen of which were painted in 1925. This sale further boosts Gris's morale.

Léonce Rosenberg's brother Paul, who is a dealer, offers contract to Gris, but he refuses.

December. Gris and Josette go for rest to southern France. Stay at the home of Mme Ollivier, near Toulon.

Day trip to Avignon; at museum there he admires a portrait attributed to the brothers Le Nain.

Raynals and Simon visit them Christmas Eve, and again to welcome in the New Year. New Year's Eve, Ford Madox Ford, the English writer who knows Gris through Stein, and his wife also join them and remain for several days.

Gris initiates procedure to obtain French citizenship.

Begins work on lithographs for *A Book Concluding With As A Wife Has A Cow A Love Story* by Gertrude Stein. Four lithographs, including one in color, are selected for the book.

Designs tapestries executed by Toklas for apartment she shares with Stein.

Ozenfant and Jeanneret publish *La peinture moderne.*

1926

Gris informs Penzol that he is studying palmistry and is learning to dance the Charleston.

January 14. Gris writes again to Kahnweiler of his pending naturalization:

> *My plan to become naturalized has produced reactions I never expected in my family. In one letter my brother criticizes me severely, and in another my sister expresses her approval. My son . . . has secretly written me a letter asking me to send for him to come and live with me. From what he says he appears to hate Spain as much as I do. As his wish is also mine, I have decided to send for him.* [*Letters,* CCXI]

January 26. Of two figure paintings of women he is working on, Gris writes to Kahnweiler, "They have a Pompeian look, but more the Pompeian look of David than of Poussin" (*Letters,* CCXII). Shortly thereafter, he comments, "Now that she is finished the woman with the drapery is more like something from Fontainebleau than from Pompeii" (*Letters,* CCXIII).

Does lithographs to illustrate the young poet Raymond Radiguet's *Denise,* to be published in March by Galerie Simon.

Health worsens; develops a fever most afternoons. Advised by Dr. Allendy not to be alarmed and to schedule a rest after lunch; this prescription temporarily alleviates Gris's concern.

February. Gris sees Ford Madox Ford and Louis Latapie, a painter, occasionally in the evening. Although they are nearby, Gris does not take the opportunity to spend time with Cocteau, Stravinsky, or Manolo. Meets Matisse's daughter, Marguerite, and her husband Georges Duthuit, the writer and Byzantinist.

Gris has bronchitis attack; tests reveal he suffers from anemia.

March. Through correspondence, advises Mme Kahnweiler on execution of needlepoint design he has done for her chairs.

March 18. Matisse visits, and Gris feels the iciness between them has worn off, informing Kahnweiler, "He was nice and not at all self-important" (*Letters*, CCXXIV).

Having finished a series of twelve paintings and not wanting to resume serious work before returning to Paris, Gris works on watercolors.

April. Returns to Boulogne-sur-Seine.

Sees Fords, among others.

Works on lithographs for Stein's forthcoming book.

July. Gris's son Georges, now seventeen years old, comes to Boulogne-sur-Seine from Madrid with Gris's sister Antonieta and her son Guillermo. At end of their several weeks' visit, Georges decides to remain with his father and Josette.

Gris injures his foot which is very swollen for much of the summer. Health improves in mid-summer, but daily feverish condition returns; he is confined to bed.

August. Doctors speculate that he may have contracted typhoid.

October 22–29. Gris is among artists who donate pictures to *Le salon du franc* at the Parisian Musée Galliéra, held to maintain the value of the French currency.

Gris informs Stein he has once again been ill and that, on the basis of x-rays, his doctors have diagnosed a weak lung. Counseled to spend winter in a mountainous region.

After further consultation with physicians, Gris and Josette believe it is not necessary for them to go to high altitudes for his recuperation, but may install themselves in the southern part of the country if it is not too near the sea.

October 28. Sale of John Quinn collection at Hôtel Drouot in Paris; contains nine paintings by Gris.

Late November. Gris, Josette, and Georges leave Boulogne-sur-Seine and install themselves at Hyères at Villa Germinal, Quartier Mont-Fleury, Route Nationale 98.

Almost immediately Georges contracts tonsilitis and runs high temperature. In nursing him Gris catches the infection and has sore throat; is concerned it will worsen.

Gris reports to Stein, Kahnweiler, and Raynal through letters that he and the others are leading a rather "sober life"— keeping regular hours, curbing all evening outings, imposing a strict diet.

December. Gris feels better and begins to work, with supplies Josette brings him from Toulon, in the studio they have arranged in their living quarters.

Gris contracts bronchitis. Also suffers from serious and frequent bouts of asthma which began with their arrival at Hyères. These attacks get increasingly acute, especially at night, preventing him from getting sleep.

Medical examination reveals Gris's blood pressure has increased despite his severe regime and strict life style. He is put on new medicine, to counteract what is diagnosed as emphysema, as well as morphine to help him cope with symptoms of asthma.

1927

January. Gris paints about three hours each morning and does some drawing in the evening. Remarks to Kahnweiler that this "monastic" life style is surprisingly tolerable.

Increased severity of asthmatic episodes.

January 22. Departs for Puget-Theniers, in the Alpes Maritimes about eighty kilometers from Nice and 500 meters above sea level, to escape supposed ill effects of Hyères on his health. New environment induces no relief; uremia is diagnosed.

January 24. Josette and Gris return hastily to Boulogne-sur-Seine.

February–May. Gris suffers three major attacks of uremia; is confined to bed with each crisis. After the initial two attacks, recovers sufficiently to return to work.

May 11. Gris dies at Boulogne-sur-Seine at the age of forty.

May 13. Burial at cemetery at Boulogne-sur-Seine.

Maurice Raynal's *Anthologie de la peinture en France de 1906 à nos jours* is published. It includes the following statement by Gris:

> *Today, at the age of forty, I believe that I am approaching a new period of self-expression, of pictorial expression, of picture-language; a well thought-out and well blended unity.* [English translation, Kahnweiler, p. 146]

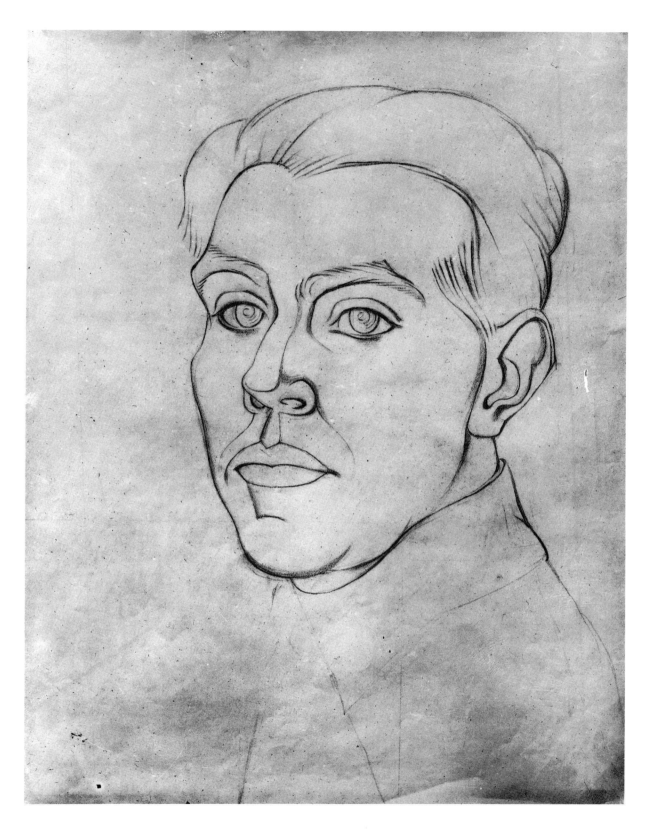

Self-portrait, 1921 (cat. 99)

Solo Exhibitions

1912 Clovis Sagot, Paris. January.

1919 Galerie de l'Effort Moderne (Léonce Rosenberg), Paris. April 5–30.

1920 Galerie Alfred Flechtheim, Düsseldorf. February 15–March 13.

1921 Galerie de l'Effort Moderne (Léonce Rosenberg), Paris. March 1–25.

1922 Galerie la Licorne (Girardin), Paris. November.

1923 Galerie Simon, Paris. March 20–April 5.
Galerie Alfred Flechtheim, Berlin. October.

1925 Galerie Alfred Flechtheim, Düsseldorf. April.

1928 Galerie Simon, Paris. June 4–16.

1930 Galerie Alfred Flechtheim, Berlin. February.

1932 Marie Harriman Gallery, New York. February.

1933 Kunsthaus, Zurich. April 2–26.

1935 Howard Putzel Gallery, San Francisco. January. Exhibition circulated to: Julien Levy Gallery, New York, October–November; The Arts Club of Chicago, December 13–30.

1936 Mayor Gallery, London. November.

1938 Galerie Roland Balaÿ and Louis Carré, Paris. June 13–July 3. Jacques Seligmann and Co., New York. November 10–December.

1939 The Arts Club of Chicago. January 3–27.

1944 Buchholz Gallery (Curt Valentin), New York. March 28–April 22.

1947 Buchholz Gallery (Curt Valentin), New York. April.

1948 Modern Art Society, Cincinnati. April 30–May 31.

1950 Buchholz Gallery (Curt Valentin), New York. January–February.

1955 Musée des Beaux-Arts, Bern. October 29–January 2.

1957 Galerie Louise Leiris, Paris. October 23–November 23.

1958 Marlborough Fine Art Ltd., London. February–March. The Museum of Modern Art, New York. April 9–June 1. Exhibition traveled to: The Minneapolis Institute of Arts, June 24–July 24; San Francisco Museum of Art, August 11–September 14; Los Angeles County Museum of Art, September 29–October 26.

1965 Galerie Louise Leiris, Paris. June 17–July 17.
Museum am Ostwall, Dortmund. October 23–December 4. Exhibition traveled to Wallraf-Richartz Museum, Cologne, December 29–February 13, 1966.

1967 Saidenberg Gallery, New York. May 9–June 24.

1968 Galleria Il Milione, Milan. March–April.
Galleria La Nuova Pesa, Rome. Galleria Obere Zäune, Zurich. November 2–December 7.

1973 Orangerie des Tuilleries, Paris. March 14–July 1.

1974 Staatliche Kunsthalle, Baden-Baden. July 20–September 29.

1977 Galeria Theo, Madrid. May–June.

Bibliography

Writings by Juan Gris

Untitled article on Cubist aesthetics [in Italian]. *Valori Plastici* (Rome, February/March 1919), p. 2. Reprinted in English in Daniel-Henry Kahnweiler. *Juan Gris: His Life and Work.* Translated by Douglas Cooper. London: Lund Humphries, 1947, p. 137 (hereafter referred to as Kahnweiler).

Untitled statement on Negro art. *Action*, no. 3 (Paris, April 1920), p. 24. Kahnweiler, p. 137.

Untitled biography of Juan Gris [signed "Vauvrecy"]. *L'Esprit Nouveau*, no. 5 (Paris, February 1921), pp. 533–534. Kahnweiler, pp. 137–138.

"Notes sur ma peinture." *Der Querschnitt*, nos. 1–2 (Frankfurt, Summer 1923), pp. 77–78.

"Des possibilités de la peinture." Originally delivered as a lecture at the Sorbonne, Paris. First appeared in English in *The Transatlantic Review* 1, no. 6 (Paris, July 1924), pp. 482–488, and ibid. 2, no. 1, pp. 78–79. Kahnweiler, pp. 139–144.

"Réponse à l'enquête 'chez les cubistes.'" *Bulletin de la Vie Artistique* 6 (Paris, January 1, 1925): 15–17. Kahnweiler, pp. 144–145.

"Antwort (auf einige fragen . . . über den Kubismus)." *Europa-Almanach* (Potsdam, 1925), pp. 34–36. Kahnweiler, pp. 145–146.

Untitled statement on p. 172 in Maurice Raynal, *Anthologie de la peinture en France de 1906 à nos jours.* Paris: Montaigne, 1927.

Letters of Juan Gris, 1913–1927. See Monographs, Douglas Cooper, ed. and trans.

Posibilidades de la pintura y otros escritos. Translated by Alfred Terzaga. Córdoba, Argentina: Editorial Assandri, 1957.

De las posibilidades da la pintura y otros escritos. Introduction by Daniel-Henry Kahnweiler; translated by J.E. Cirlot. Letras de Arte. Barcelona: Editorial Gustavo Gili, 1971.

Books illustrated by Juan Gris

Santos Chocano, José. *Alma América, Poemas indoespañoles.* Madrid: Victoriano Suárez, 1906.

Reverdy, Pierre. *Poèmes en prose.* Paris: Paul Birault, 1915.

Huidobro, Vicente. *Horizon carré: Poèmes.* Paris: Paul Birault, 1917.

Reverdy, Pierre. *La guitare endormie.* Paris: Nord-Sud, 1919.

Huidobro, Vicente. *Tremblement de ciel.* Paris: Louis Tscham, undated.

Dermée. Paul. *Beautés de 1918.* Paris: "Editions de L'Esprit Nouveau," 1919.

Jacob, Max. *Ne coupez pas mademoiselle ou les erreurs des P.T.T..* Paris: Galerie Simon, 1921.

Salacrou, Armand. *Le casseur d'assiettes.* Paris: Galerie Simon, 1924.

Peiper, Tadeusz. *Żywe linje.* Cracow: n.p., 1924.

Tzara, Tristan. *Mouchoir de nuages.* Paris: Galerie Simon, 1925.

Radiguet, Raymond. *Denise.* Paris: Galerie Simon, 1926.

Stein, Gertrude. *A Book Concluding With As A Wife Has A Cow: A Love Story.* Paris: Galerie Simon, 1926.

Reverdy, Pierre. *Au soleil du plafond.* Paris: Tériade, 1956.

Monographs

Cooper, Douglas. *Juan Gris ou le goût du solennel.* Geneva: Skira, 1949.

————, ed. and trans. *Letters of Juan Gris, 1913–1927.* Collected by Daniel-Henry Kahnweiler. London: privately printed, 1956.

————. *Juan Gris: Catalogue raisonné de l'oeuvre peint établi avec la collaboration de Margaret Potter.* 2 vols. Paris: Berggruen, 1977.

————. See Exhibition Catalogues, Bern.

Gaya-Nuño, Juan Antonio. *Juan Gris.* Translated by Kenneth Lyons. London: Secker & Warburg, 1975.

George, Waldemar. *Juan Gris: Peintres nouveaux.* Paris: Gallimard, 1931.

Henry, Daniel [pseud.]. See Daniel-Henry Kahnweiler.

Kahnweiler, Daniel-Henry. *Juan Gris.* Leipzig and Berlin: Klinkhardt & Biermann, 1929.

———. *Juan Gris, His Life and Work.* Translated by Douglas Cooper. London: Lund Humphries; New York: Curt Valentin, 1947. Rev. ed. New York: Abrams, 1969.

Raynal, Maurice. *Juan Gris, vingt tableaux.* Les maîtres du cubisme, 1st series. Paris: Editions de l'Effort Moderne, Léonce Rosenberg, 1920.

Schmidt, Georg. *Juan Gris und die Geschichte des Kubismus.* Baden-Baden: Woldemar Klein, 1957.

Sterup-Hansen, Dan, ed. *Juan Gris: Et Foredrag.* Copenhagen: Wivel, 1946.

Exhibition Catalogues

Baden-Baden. Kunsthalle. *Juan Gris*, texts by Jean Leymarie, Man Ray, Gertrude Stein, Daniel-Henry Kahnweiler, Will Grohmann, Georg Schmidt, Joachim Büchner, Herta Wescher, and reprinted writings by Juan Gris, 1974.

Barcelona. Galerias Dalmau. *Cubistas (Exposición d'arte cubista)*, introduction in French by Jacques Nayral, 1912.

Basel. Galerie Beyeler. *Le cubisme: Braque, Gris, Léger, Picasso*, introduction in German by Georg Schmidt, 1962.

Basel. Galerie Beyeler. *Spanish Artists. Gris, Picasso, Miró, Chillida, Tàpies*, 1969.

Berlin. Galerie Alfred Flechtheim. *Gedaechtnisausstellung Juan Gris*, essay by Gertrude Stein, 1930.

Bern. Kunstmuseum. *Juan Gris*, by Douglas Cooper, 1955.

Bordeaux. Galerie des Beaux Arts. *Les cubistes*, essays by G. Martin-Mery, Jacques Lassaigne, Jean Cassou, 1973.

Brooklyn Museum. *International Exhibition of Modern Art*, by Katherine S. Dreier, 1926.

Dortmund. Museum am Ostwall. *Juan Gris*, foreword by John Richardson, introduction by Daniel-Henry Kahnweiler, text by L. Reygers, 1965.

Düsseldorf. Galerie Alfred Flechtheim. *Auf dem Wege zur Kunst unserer Zeit*, introduction by Alfred Flechtheim, 1919.

Düsseldorf. Galerie Alfred Flechtheim. *Juan Gris*, 1920.

Düsseldorf. *Internationale Kunstaustellung*, 1922.

Frankfurt. Kunstverein. *Neue französische Malerei*, 1926.

Geneva. Galerie Moos. *La jeune peinture française: Les cubistes*, introduction by Léonce Rosenberg, 1920.

London. Marlborough Fine Art Ltd. *Juan Gris 1887–1927, Retrospective Exhibition*, prefaces by Daniel-Henry Kahnweiler and John Russell, 1958.

Los Angeles County Museum of Art. *The Cubist Epoch*, by Douglas Cooper, 1970.

Lyons. Exhibition arranged by the magazine *Promenoir*, introduction by Henri Focillon, 1921.

Madrid. Galeria Theo. *Juan Gris*, 1977.

Milan. Galleria Il Milione. *Juan Gris*, preface by Daniel-Henry Kahnweiler, 1968.

New York. Buchholz Gallery (Curt Valentin). *Juan Gris 1887–1927*, preface by Jacques Lipchitz, reprint of statements by Juan Gris, 1944.

New York. The Museum of Modern Art. *Cubism and Abstract Art*, by Alfred Barr, 1936.

New York. The Museum of Modern Art. *Juan Gris*, by James Thrall Soby, 1958.

New York. The Museum of Modern Art. *Four Americans in Paris*, 1970.

New York. Saidenberg Gallery. *Juan Gris: Drawings and Gouaches 1910–1927*, preface by Daniel-Henry Kahnweiler, 1967.

Paris. Galerie La Boétie. *La section d'or*, preface by R. Blum, 1912.

Paris. Galerie de France. *Le cubisme*, preface by B. Dorival, 1945.

Paris. Galerie des Beaux-Arts. *Les créateurs du cubisme*, by Raymond Cogniat, 1935.

Paris. Galerie Louise Leiris. *L'atelier de Juan Gris*, preface by Daniel-Henry Kahnweiler, 1957.

Paris. Galerie Louise Leiris. *50 ans d'édition de D.-H. Kahnweiler*, by Jean Hugues, 1959.

Paris. Galerie Louise Leiris. *Juan Gris: Dessins et gouaches 1910–1927*, preface by Daniel-Henry Kahnweiler, 1965.

Paris. Galerie Roland Balaÿ and Louis Carré. *L'oeuvre de Juan Gris*, essays by Maurice Raynal, Gertrude Stein, and Douglas Lord [Douglas Cooper], 1938.

Paris. Galerie Simon. *Juan Gris*, introduction by Maurice Raynal, 1923.

Paris. M. Knoedler & Co. *Le cubisme: Picasso, Braque, Gris, Léger*, essay by Christian Zervos, slightly altered version of Galerie Beyeler, Basel, 1962.

Paris. Musée Galliera. *Le salon du franc*, 1926.

Paris. Musée National d'Art Moderne. *Le cubisme*, by G. Vienne, preface by Jean Cassou, 1953.

Paris. Musée National d'Art Moderne. *Les sources de XXe siècle*, prefaces by Jean Cassou, J. C. Argan, Nikolaus Pevsner, 1960.

Paris. Musée National d'Art Moderne. *A la rencontre de Pierre Reverdy et ses amis: Picasso, Braque, Laurens, Gris, Léger, Matisse, Modigliani, Manolo, Gargallo, Derain, Chagall, Giacometti, Miró*, 1970.

Paris. Petit Palais. *Les maîtres de l'art indépendant 1895-1937*, 1936.

Paris. Réunion des Musées Nationaux. *Juan Gris*, preface by Jean Leymarie, reprint of writings by Juan Gris, 1974.

Rouen. Société de Peinture Moderne. *Exposition*, introduction by Elie Faure and Maurice Raynal, 1912.

San Francisco Museum of Art. *Picasso, Gris, Miró: The Spanish Masters of 20th-Century Painting*, texts by Donald Gallup, Juan Larrea, Man Ray, Sidney Janis, Daniel-Henry Kahnweiler, Herbert Read, and reprints of statements by Juan Gris, Pablo Picasso, and Joan Miró, 1948.

Venice. 25th Biennale. *Quattro maestri del cubismo*, preface by Douglas Cooper, 1950.

Venice, 28th Biennale. *Juan Gris*, text by Daniel-Henry Kahnweiler, 1956, pp. 250-253.

Zurich. Galerie Obere Zäune. *Juan Gris*, 1968.

Zurich. Kunsthaus. *Juan Gris*, preface by W. Wartmann, 1933.

Zurich. Salon d'Art Wolfsberg. *Exhibition of French Graphic Art*, 1923.

Articles

Acatos, Sylvio. "Architecture et émotion." *Oeil* 227: 32-37.
Apollinaire, Guillaume. "Chez le peintre Juan Gris." *Mercure de France*, Paris, 16 February 1912, p. 888.
———. "À *La section d'or*," *L'Intransigeant*, 10 October 1912.
———. "Le salon des indépendants," *L'Intransigeant*, 25 March 1912.
Arte Vivo (Valencia, May/June 1959). Issue dedicated to Juan Gris.

Brugière, P.G. "La présence de Juan Gris." *Cahiers d'Art* 26 (Paris, 1951): 115-36.
Bulletin de l'Effort Moderne, Paris.
Cahiers d'Art 8, nos. 5-6 (Paris, 1933). Issue dedicated to Juan Gris and Fernand Léger.
Camfield, William A. "Juan Gris and the Golden Section." *The Art Bulletin* 47 (March 1965): 128-34.
Carmean, Jr., E.A. "Juan Gris' 'Fantômas.'" *Arts* 51, no. 5 (January 1977), pp. 116-19.
Cooper, Douglas. "The Temperament of Juan Gris." *The Metropolitan Museum of Art Bulletin* (April 1971), pp. 358-62.
——— [Douglas Lord]. "Juan Gris," *Axis*, no. 7 (London, Autumn 1936), pp. 9-12.
Eluard, Paul. "Juan Gris" [poem]. *Voir: Poèmes, peintres, dessins*, Geneva: Editions des Trois Collines [ca. 1948], pp. 154-61.
L'Esprit Nouveau, Paris.
Figuerola-Ferretti, Luis. "Juan Gris y el cubismo hoy." *Goya* 138 (May/June 1977): 354-59.
George, Waldemar. "Juan Gris." *L'Amour de l'Art* 2, no. 11 (November 1921), pp. 351-52.
Green, Christopher. "A Spaniard's Interpretation of Juan Gris." *Apollo* (March 1976), pp. 248-49.
———. "Synthesis and the 'Synthetic Process' in the Painting of Juan Gris 1915-19." *Art History* 5, no. 1 (March 1982), pp. 87-105.
———. "Purity, Poetry and the Painting of Juan Gris." *Art History* 5, no. 2 (June 1982), pp. 180-204.
Habasque, Guy. "L'atelier de Juan Gris." *Oeil* 37 (January 1958): 28-35.
Huggler, Max. "Bemerkungen zum Werk von Juan Gris." In *Festschrift Kurt Bach*. Deutscher Kunstverlag, 1957.
Kahnweiler, Daniel-Henry. "Der Tod des Juan Gris." *Der Querschnitt* 7 (July 1927): 558.
Kramer, Hilton. "Month in Review." *Arts* 32, no. 8 (May 1958), pp. 48-51.
L., H.A. "A Note on Juan Gris and Cubism," *Broom* 5, no. 1 (New York, August 1923), pp. 32-35.
La Brosse. "Silhouettes: Juan Gris." *Paris-Journal*, 22 July 1912.

The Little Review (New York, Autumn/Winter 1923-24; Autumn/Winter 1924-25, issue devoted to Juan Gris).
Lord, Douglas. See Douglas Cooper.
Lyons, Lisa. "Matisse: Work 1914-1917." *Arts* 49, no. 9 (May 1975), pp. 74-75.
[Ozenfant, Amédée.] "Juan Gris" [signed "Vauvrecy"]. *L'Esprit Nouveau* 5 (February 1921): 533-34. See Writings by Juan Gris.
Paul, Eliot. "A Master of Plastic Relations." *Transition* 4 (New York, July 1927): 163-65.
Ray, Man. "Juan Gris—Joan Miró—Pablo Picasso." See Exhibition Catalogues, San Francisco Museum of Art.
Raynal, Maurice. "L'exposition de 'La section d'or.'" *La Section d'Or* (Paris, 1912), pp. 2-5.
———. "Juan Gris." *L'Esprit Nouveau* 1, no. 5 (February 1921), pp. 533-55.
———. "Juan Gris." *Bulletin de l'Effort Moderne* (June 1925), pp. 1-16.
———. "Juan Gris et la métaphore plastique." *Les Feuilles Libres* 5, no. 31 (March/April 1923), pp. 63-65.
Reverdy, Pierre. "Sur le Cubisme." *Nord-Sud* 1 (March 15, 1917): 5-7.
Read, Herbert. "The Literature of Art: Juan Gris." *The Burlington Magazine* 90, no. 539 (February 1948), p. 52.
Rosenblum, Robert. "Picasso and the Typography of Cubism." In *Picasso in Retrospect*, edited by Sir Roland Penrose and Dr. John Golding. New York: Praeger, 1973.
Salmon, André. "Juan Gris." *Paris-Journal*, 21 January 1912.
Schmidt, Georg. "Juan Gris." *Das Kunstwerk* 11, no. 7 (January 1958), pp. 3-14.
Seligman, Ethlyne J., and Seligman, Germain. "Of the Proximity of Death and its Stylistic Activations—Roger de la Fresnaye and Juan Gris." *Art Quarterly* 12, no. 2, (Spring 1949), pp. 147-55.
Stein, Gertrude. "The Life of Juan Gris, The Life and Death of Juan Gris." In *Portraits and Prayers*. New York: Random House, 1935.
———. "Pictures of Juan Gris." In *Portraits and Prayers*. New York: Random House, 1935.

—. See *The Little Review*, 1924–25, p. 16.

Strauss, Ernst. "Über Juan Gris 'Technique Picturale.'" In *Amici Amico: Festschrift für Werner Gross*. Munich: W. Fink, 1968.

Tériade, E. "Juan Gris." *Cahiers d'Art* 3 nos. 5–6 (1928), pp. 213–46.

Torres-García, Joaquín. "Juan Gris y el cubismo" [text dated August 1936]. In *Universalismo Constructivo*. Buenos Aires: Editorial Poseidon, 1944.

Vicente, Esteban. "Gris: Reality Cubed." *Art News* 57, no. 3 (May 1958), pp. 30–33.

Young, Vernon. "London," *Arts* 32, no. 7 (April 1958), pp. 22–23.

Zervos, Christian. "Juan Gris et l'inquiétude d'aujourd'hui." *Cahiers d'Art* 1, no. 10 (1926), pp. 269–74.

Z[ervos], C[hristian]. "Juan Gris." *Cahiers d'Art* 2, nos. 4–5 (1927), pp. 170–72.

General books

Abel, Ulf, ed. *The Grace and Philip Sandblom Collection*. Stockholm: Nationalmuseum, 1981.

Apollinaire, Guillaume. *Chroniques d'art (1902–1918)*. Paris: Gallimard, 1960. English edition *Apollinaire on Art*, London and New York: Viking, 1972.

Apollinaire, Guillaume. *Les peintres cubistes: Meditations esthétiques*. Paris: Figuière, 1913. English translation by Lionel Abel. *The Cubist Painters: Aesthetic Meditations*. The Documents of Modern Art, vol. 1. New York: George Wittenborn, 1962.

Barr, Jr., Alfred H. See Exhibition Catalogues, New York, The Museum of Modern Art, 1936 and 1964.

Cogniat, Raymond. See Exhibition Catalogues, Paris, Galerie des Beaux-Arts.

Cooper, Douglas. See Exhibition Catalogues, Los Angeles.

Berger, John. *Permanent Red*. London and New York: Writers and Readers Publishing Cooperative, 1981.

Dreier, Katherine S. See Exhibition Catalogues, Brooklyn.

Fry, Edward F. *Cubism*. London: Thames & Hudson, 1966.

Gamwell, Lynn. *Cubist Criticism*. Studies on the Fine Arts: Criticism, vol. 5. Ann Arbor: UMI Research Press, 1980.

Gleizes, Albert and Metzinger, Jean. *Du cubisme*. Paris: Figuière, 1912; and London: Unwin, 1913.

Gleizes, Albert, and Metzinger, Jean. *Du* Langen, 1928.

Golding, John. *Cubism: A History and an Analysis, 1907–1914*. New York: George Wittenborn, 1959.

Gordon, Donald E. *Modern Art Exhibitions 1900–1916*. 2 vols. Munich: Prestel, 1974.

Gray, Christopher. *Cubist Aesthetic Theories*. Baltimore: Johns Hopkins Press, 1953.

Green, Christopher. *Léger and the Avant-Garde*. New Haven and London: Yale University Press, 1976.

Hugues, Jean. See Exhibition Catalogues, Paris, Galerie Louis Leiris.

Jardot, Maurice, and Martin, Kurt. *Die Meister französischer Malerei der Gegenwart*. Baden-Baden: Woldemar Klein, 1948.

Judkins, Winthrop Otis. *Fluctuant Representation in Synthetic Cubism: Picasso, Braque, Gris, 1910–1920*. Ph.D. dissertation, Harvard University, 1954. Outstanding Dissertations in the Fine Arts. New York and London: Garland, 1976.

Kahnweiler, Daniel-Henry, with Crémieux, Francis. *My Galleries and Painters*. Translated by Helen Weaver. Introduction by John Russell. The Documents of 20th-Century Art. New York: Viking, 1971.

Ozenfant, Amédée. *Foundations of Modern Art*. New York: Brewer, Warren & Putnam, 1931. French edition first appeared in 1929. Paris: Budry.

—. Mémoires *1886–1962*. Paris: Seghers, 1968.

Penrose, Sir Roland, and Golding, Dr. John, eds. *Picasso in Retrospect*. New York: Praeger, 1973.

Raynal, Maurice. *Anthologie de la peinture en France de 1906 à nos jours*. Paris: Montaigne, 1927.

—. *From Picasso to Surrealism*. History of Modern Painting, vol. 3. Geneva: Skira, 1950.

—. *Modern Painting*. Translated by Stuart Gilbert. Geneva: Skira, 1953.

—. *Peintres du XXe siècle*. Geneva: Skira, 1947.

—. *Quelques intentions du cubisme*. Paris: Editions de l'Effort Moderne, 1919.

Rosenblum, Robert, *Cubism and Twentieth-Century Art*. New York: Abrams, 1960.

Salmon, André. *L'art vivant*, Paris: Crès, 1920.

—. *La jeune peinture française*. Paris: Messein, 1912.

Severini, Gino. *Tutta la vita di un pittore*, vol. 1. Rome and Paris: Garzanti, 1946.

Stein, Gertrude. *Lectures in America*. New York: Random House, 1935.

—. *The Autobiography of Alice B. Toklas*. New York: Harcourt, Brace, and Company, 1933.

—. *Picasso*. London: B.T. Batsford, Ltd., 1948.

Catalogue of the Exhibition

Titles and dates conform to the catalogue raisonné by Douglas Cooper (listed in the Bibliography). In cases where two titles are given for a single entry, however, the first is the title used by the lender, the second that assigned by Cooper. Media and dimensions follow Cooper except where revised information has been provided by lenders. Dimensions are given in centimeters followed by inches in parentheses, height preceding width. A number following the letters "DC" refers to the corresponding entry in the catalogue raisonné; it is included as a guide for the reader seeking further exhibition and provenance information.

Works on Canvas and Wood

1 *Siphon and Bottles*, 1910
Oil on cardboard, transferred to canvas
57 x 48 cm. (22½ x 18⅞ in.)
Georges Gonzalez-Gris Collection
(DC 1)

2 *The Book*, 1911
Oil on canvas
55 x 46 cm. (21⅝ x 18⅛ in.)
Private collection, Paris
(DC 3)

3 *Bottle and Pitcher*, 1911
Oil on canvas
55 x 33 cm. (21⅝ x 13 in.)
Rijksmuseum Kröller-Müller, Otterlo, Netherlands
(DC 6)

4 *Houses in Paris*, 1911
Oil on canvas
52.4 x 34.3 cm. (20⅝ x 13½ in.)
The Solomon R. Guggenheim Museum, New York
(DC 7)

5 *Houses in Paris—Place Ravignan*, 1911
Oil on canvas
52 x 34 cm. (20½ x 13⅜ in.)
Private collection
(DC 9)

6 *Portrait of Picasso*, 1912
Oil on canvas
93.4 x 74.3 cm. (36¾ x 29¼ in.)
The Art Institute of Chicago
Gift of Leigh B. Block
(DC 13)

7 *Portrait of the Artist's Mother*, 1912
Oil on canvas
55 x 46 cm. (21⅝ x 18⅛ in.)
Private collection
(DC 14)
[New York only]

8 *Still Life with Oil Lamp*, 1912
Oil on canvas
48 x 33 cm. (18⅞ x 13 in.)
Rijksmuseum Kröller-Müller, Otterlo, Netherlands
(DC 15)

9 *Banjo and Glasses*, 1912
Oil on canvas
30 x 58 cm. (11⅞ x 22⅞ in.)
Mr. and Mrs. Morton G. Neumann Collection
(DC 21)

10 *Man in the Café (Man at Café)*, 1912
Oil on canvas
128 x 88 cm. (50⅜ x 34⅝ in.)
Philadelphia Museum of Art
The Louise and Walter Arensberg Collection
(DC 25)
[Berkeley only]

11 *The Watch*, 1912
Oil and *papier collé* on canvas
65 x 92 cm. (25⅝ x 36¼ in.)
Private collection
(DC 27)

12 *Glass of Beer and Playing Cards*, 1913
Oil and *papier collé* on canvas
52.5 x 36.5 cm. (20⅝ x 14⅜ in.)
Columbus Museum of Art, Ohio
Gift of Ferdinand Howald
(DC 35)

13 *Guitar on Table*, 1913
Oil on canvas
73 x 60 cm. (28¾ x 23⅝ in.)
Mr. and Mrs. Roy J. Friedman Collection
(DC 36)
[Washington and Berkeley only]

14 *The Siphon*, 1913
Oil on canvas
81 x 65 cm. (31⅞ x 25⅝ in.)
Rose Art Museum, Brandeis University, Waltham, Massachusetts
Gift of Edgar Kaufman, Jr., New York
(DC 37)

15 *Untitled (Violin and Ink Bottle on a Table)*, 1913
Oil on canvas
89.5 x 60.5 cm. (35¼ x 23⅞ in.)
Kunstsammlung Nordrhein-Westfalen, Düsseldorf
(DC 39)

16 *The Guitar*, 1913
Oil and *papier collé* on canvas
61 x 50 cm. (24 x 19⅝ in.)
Private collection, Paris
(DC 42)

17 *The Bottle of Claret*, 1913
Oil and *papier collé* on canvas
55 x 33 cm. (21⅝ x 13 in.)
Private collection
(DC 43)

18 *Landscape with Houses at Céret*, 1913
Oil on canvas
100 x 65 cm. (39⅜ x 25⅝ in.)
Galeria Theo, Madrid
(DC 56)

19 *Violin and Guitar*, 1913
Oil on canvas
100 x 65.5 cm. (39⅜ x 25¾ in.)
The Colin Collection, New York
Property of Ralph F. Colin, Jr.
(DC 57)
[New York only]

20 *Violin and Checkerboard*, 1913
Oil on canvas
100 x 65 cm. (39⅜ x 25⅝ in.)
Stephen A. Simon and Bonnie Simon
Collection
(DC 60)

21 *Pears and Grapes on a Table*, 1913
Oil on canvas
54.5 x 73 cm. (21½ x 28¾ in.)
Mr. and Mrs. Burton Tremaine Collection,
Meriden, Connecticut
(DC 61)

22 *The Man at the Café*, 1914
Oil and *papier collé* on canvas
99 x 72 cm. (39 x 28⅜ in.)
Acquavella Galleries, Inc., New York
(DC 76)

23 *Musician's Table*, 1914
Fusain, graphite, and colored pencil
on *paper collé* on canvas
81 x 59.5 cm. (31⅞ x 23½ in.)
Private collection, New York
(DC 84)
[Washington only]

24 *The Newspaper (Cup, Glasses, and Bottle)*, 1914
Oil, *papier collé*, and pencil on canvas
55 x 46 cm. (21⅝ x 18⅛ in.)
Judith Rothschild Collection
(DC 89)

25 *Guitar, Glasses, and Bottle*, 1914
Papier collé, gouache, and fusain on canvas
60 x 81 cm. (23⅝ x 31⅞ in.)
National Gallery of Ireland, Dublin
(DC 94)

26 *The Glass*, 1914
Papier collé, pencil, and gouache on canvas
39.5 x 41 cm. (15½ x 16⅛ in.)
Perls Galleries, New York
(DC 110)

27 *Bottle of Banyul (Bottle and Glass)*, 1914
Papier collé, oil, and pencil on board
38 x 28.5 cm. (15 x 11¼ in.)
Mr. and Mrs. James W. Aldsdorf
Collection, Chicago
(DC 111)

28 *The Guitar*, 1914
Papier collé, gouache, fusain, and
pencil on canvas
65 x 46 cm. (25⅝ x 18⅛ in.)
Private collection
(DC 118)

29 *Violin and Glass*, 1915
Oil on canvas
92 x 60 cm. (36¼ x 23⅝ in.)
Fogg Art Museum, Harvard University,
Cambridge, Massachusetts
Gift of Mr. and Mrs. Joseph Pulitzer, Jr.
(DC 122)
[Washington and Berkeley only]

30 *Still Life with Checked Tablecloth*, 1915
Oil on canvas
116 x 89 cm. (45⅝ x 35 in.)
Private collection
(DC 127)
[Washington only]

31 *Book, Pipe, and Glasses*, 1915
Oil on canvas
73 x 91.5 cm. (28¾ x 36 in.)
The Colin Collection, New York
Property of Lady Harlech
(DC 128)
[New York only]

32 *Still Life*, 1915
Oil on canvas
116 x 90 cm. (45⅝ x 35⅜ in.)
Staatliche Museen Preussischer
Kulturbesitz,
Nationalgalerie, Berlin
(DC 130)

33 *Still Life before an Open Window:
Place Ravignan (Still Life and Landscape—
Place Ravignan)*, 1915
Oil on canvas
116 x 89 cm. (45⅝ x 35 in.)
Philadelphia Museum of Art
The Louise and Walter Arensberg
Collection
(DC 131)
[Washington and New York only]

34 *The Cherries*, 1915
Oil on canvas
55 x 38 cm. (21⅝ x 15 in.)
Richard S. Zeisler Collection, New York
(DC 141)

35 *The Pot of Geraniums*, 1915
Oil on canvas
81 x 60 cm. (31⅞ x 23⅝ in.)
Collection S
(DC 144)

36 *Fantômas (Pipe and Newspaper)*,
1915
Oil on canvas
59.8 x 73.3 cm. (23½ x 28⅞ in.)
National Gallery of Art, Washington, D.C.
Chester Dale Fund, 1976
(DC 146)

37 *The Breakfast Table*, 1915
Oil on canvas
92 x 73 cm. (36¼ x 28¾ in.)
Musée National d'Art Moderne,
Centre Georges Pompidou, Paris
(DC 149)

38 *Guitar on a Table*, 1915
Oil on canvas
73 x 92 cm. (28¾ x 36¼ in.)
Rijksmuseum Kröller-Müller, Otterlo, Netherlands
(DC 150)

39 *The Newspaper (Glass and Newspaper)*, 1916
Oil on canvas
41 x 33 cm. (16⅛ x 13 in.)
Private collection, Paris
(DC 156)

40 *Newspaper and Fruit Dish*, 1916
Oil on canvas
96 x 60 cm. (36¼ x 23⅝ in.)
Yale University Art Gallery
Gift of Collection Société Anonyme
(DC 161)
[Washington only]

41 *Fruit Dish and Bottle*, 1916
Oil on canvas
65 x 80.5 cm. (25⅝ x 31⅞ in.)
Smith College Museum of Art, Northampton, Massachusetts
Gift of Joseph Brummer, 1921
(DC 165)

42 *Head of a Man—Self-portrait*, 1916
Oil on canvas
63 x 48.5 cm. (24⅞ x 19⅛ in.)
Private collection
(DC 170)
[Washington and Berkeley only]

43 *The Siphon*, 1916
Oil on canvas
55 x 46.5 cm. (21⅝ x 18⅜ in.)
Museum Ludwig, Cologne
(DC 171)

44 *Hot Water Jug and Bowl*, 1916
Oil on canvas
81 x 45 cm. (31⅞ x 17⅝ in.)
James Johnson Sweeney Collection
(DC 172)

45 *Water Bottle and Newspaper*, 1916
Oil and pencil on panel
46 x 65 cm. (18⅛ x 25⅝ in.)
Norton Gallery of Art, West Palm Beach, Florida
(DC 177)

46 *Fruit Dish, Glass, and Newspaper*, 1916
Oil on panel
56 x 31 cm. (22 x 12¼ in.)
Private collection
(DC 180)
[Washington and Berkeley only]

47 *Fruit Dish, Glass, and Lemon (Still Life with Newspaper)*, 1916
Oil on canvas
73 x 60 cm. (28¾ x 23⅝ in.)
The Phillips Collection, Washington, D.C.
(DC 188)
[Washington and Berkeley only]

48 *The Violin*, 1916
Oil on plywood
79.5 x 53.5 cm. (31¼ x 21 in.)
Private collection
(DC 190)

49 *Portrait of Josette Gris*, 1916
Oil on panel
116 x 73 cm. (45⅝ x 28¾ in.)
Museo del Prado (Casón del Buen Retiro), Madrid
(DC 203)

50 *Still Life (Bottle and Fruit Dish)*, 1917
Oil on panel
73.5 x 91.5 cm. (29 x 36 in.)
The Minneapolis Institute of Arts
The John R. Van Derlip Fund
(DC 216)

51 *Still Life (Bottle and Glass)*, 1917
Oil on panel
46 x 27 cm. (18⅛ x 10⅝ in.)
Munson-Williams-Proctor Institute, Utica, New York
(DC 233)

52 *Harlequin with a Guitar*, 1917
Oil on panel
100 x 65 cm. (39⅜ x 25⅝ in.)
Alex Hillman Family Foundation
(DC 241)

53 *Guitar, Glass, and Water Bottle*, 1917
Oil on canvas
73 x 92 cm. (28¾ x 36¼ in.)
Private collection
(DC 243)
[New York only]

54 *Still Life with Plaque*, 1917
Oil on canvas
81 x 65.5 cm. (31⅞ x 25¾ in.)
Kunstmuseum Basel
(DC 244)
[Washington only]

55 *Fruit Dish and Playing Cards*, 1918
Oil on canvas
81 x 65 cm. (31⅞ x 25⅝ in.)
Private collection
(DC 247)

56 *Violin and Glass*, 1918
Oil on canvas
80.5 x 65 cm. (31¾ x 25⅝ in.)
Katherine Urquhart Warren Collection
(DC 253)

57 *The Guitar*, 1918
Oil on canvas
81 x 60 cm. (31⅞ x 23⅝ in.)
Galerie Jan Krugier, Geneva
(DC 256)

58 *Harlequin at Table*, 1919
Oil on canvas
101 x 65 cm. (39¾ x 25⅝ in.)
Mr. and Mrs. Morton Neumann Collection
(DC 308)

59 *Guitar and Fruit Dish*, 1919
Oil on canvas
92 x 73.5 cm. (36¼ x 29 in.)
Sonja Henie-Niels Onstad Foundations, Høvikodden, Norway
(DC 310)

60 *Harlequin with Guitar (Seated Harlequin with Guitar)*, 1919
Oil on canvas
116 x 89 cm. (45⅝ x 35 in.)
Galerie Louise Leiris, Paris
(DC 321)

61 *Guitar and Fruit Dish*, 1919
Oil on canvas
60 x 73 cm. (23⅝ x 28¾ in.)
Jerome H. Stone Collection, Chicago
(DC 322)
[Washington and Berkeley only]

62 *Guitar, Book, and Newspaper*, 1920
Oil on canvas
92 x 73 cm. (36¼ x 28¾ in.)
Kunstmuseum Basel
(DC 327)

63 *Fruit Dish and Newspaper*, 1920
Oil on canvas
60 x 73 cm. (23⅝ x 28¾ in.)
Carlos Sobrino Collection, Spain
(DC 328)

64 *Still Life*
(Guitar, Pipe, and Sheets of Music), 1920
Oil on canvas
81 x 65 cm. (31⅞ x 25⅝ in.)
Van Abbemuseum, Eindhoven,
Netherlands
(DC 330)

65 *Guitar and Clarinet*, 1920
Oil on canvas
73 x 92 cm. (28¾ x 36¼ in.)
Kunstmuseum Basel
(DC 332)

66 *Guitar and Fruit Dish*, 1920
Oil on canvas
65 x 92 cm. (25⅝ x 36¼ in.)
Private collection, Basel
(DC 350)

67 *The Open Window*, 1921
Oil on canvas
65 x 100 cm. (25⅝ x 39⅜ in.)
M. Meyer Collection, Zurich
(DC 365)

68 *The View across the Bay*, 1921
Oil on canvas
65 x 100 cm. (25⅝ x 39⅜ in.)
Private collection, Paris
(DC 369)

69 *Guitar and Fruit Dish*, 1921
Oil on canvas
61 x 95 cm. (24 x 37⅜ in.)
Renée Gonzalez-Gris Collection
(DC 381)

70 *The Mountain "Le Canigou,"* 1921
Oil on canvas
65 x 100 cm. (25⅝ x 39⅜ in.)
Albright-Knox Art Gallery, Buffalo
Room of Contemporary Art Fund, 1947
(DC 384)

71 *The Book of Music*, 1922
Oil on canvas
96 x 61.5 cm. (37¾ x 24¼ in.)
Marisa del Re Gallery, New York
(DC 395)

72 *Pierrot*, 1922
Oil on canvas
100 x 65 cm. (39⅜ x 25⅝ in.)
Galerie Louise Leiris, Paris
(DC 396)

73 *Seated Harlequin*, 1923
Oil on canvas
73 x 92 cm. (28¾ x 36¼ in.)
Wadsworth Atheneum, Hartford
Lent by Carey Walker Foundation
(DC 418)

74 *Woman with Scarf*
(Woman with Handkerchief around Neck),
1924
Oil on canvas
41 x 29 cm. (16⅛ x 11½ in.)
Sonja Henie-Niels Onstad Foundations,
Høvikodden, Norway
(DC 458)

75 *The Blue Cloth*, 1925
Oil on canvas
81 x 100 cm. (31⅞ x 39⅜ in.)
Musée National d'Art Moderne,
Centre Georges Pompidou, Paris
Gift of M. et Mme A. Lefèvre
(DC 530)
[Washington only]

76 *The Open Book*, 1925
Oil on canvas
73 x 92 cm. (28¾ x 36¼ in.)
Kunstmuseum Bern
Hermann and Margrit Rupf Foundation
(DC 535)

77 *The Painter's Window*, 1925
Oil on canvas
100 x 81 cm. (39⅜ x 31⅞ in.)
The Baltimore Museum of Art, Maryland
Bequest of Sadie A. May
(DC 543)

78 *The Musician's Table*, 1926
Oil on canvas
81 x 100 cm. (31⅞ x 39⅜ in.)
Davlyn Gallery, New York
(DC 559)

79 *The Table with the Red Cloth*, 1926
Oil on canvas
92 x 73 cm. (36¼ x 28¾ in.)
Washington University Gallery of Art,
Saint Louis
(DC 586)

80 *Guitar and Music Paper*, 1926–27
Oil on canvas
65 x 81 cm. (25⅝ x 31⅞ in.)
Saidenberg Gallery, New York
(DC 608)

81 *Fruit Dish and Book*, 1927
Oil on canvas
33 x 47 cm. (13 x 18½ in.)
Private collection
(DC 613)

82 *Woman with a Basket*, 1927
Oil on canvas
92 x 73 cm. (36¼ x 28¾ in.)
Private collection
(DC 621)

Works on Paper

83 *Self-portrait*, 1910
Fusain on paper
48 x 31.3 cm. (18⅞ x 12⅜ in.)
Judith Rothschild Collection

84 *Self-portrait*, 1910–11
Pencil on paper
48 x 31.2 cm. (18⅞ x 12¼ in.)
Walter Feilchenfeldt, Zurich

85 *Cup and Glass*, 1911
Pencil on paper
34.5 x 31 cm. (13½ x 12¼ in.)
Private collection

86 *Head of a Woman*, 1911
Fusain on paper
48.2 x 31.5 cm. (19 x 12⅜ in.)
Kunstmuseum Basel, Kupferstichkabinett

87 *Flowers in a Vase*, 1911–12
Charcoal on paper
49.5 x 30.5 cm. (19½ x 12 in.)
Indiana University Art Museum,
Bloomington
Jane and Roger Wolcott Memorial
[Berkeley only]

88 *Self-portrait*, 1912
Fusain on paper
44.5 x 29 cm. (17½ x 11⅜ in.)
Private collection, Switzerland

89 *Study for "The Smoker,"* 1912
Colored charcoal on paper
72 x 59 cm. (28⅜ x 23¼ in.)
Rolf and Margit Weinberg Collection,
Switzerland

90 *Study for "Man in the Café,"* 1912
Charcoal on paper
48.3 x 31.8 cm. (19 x 12½ in.)
Private collection
(DC 25a)

91 *Coffee Grinder, Cup, and Glass on a Table*, 1915
Gouache and fusain on paper with text
glued below
30 x 21.5 cm. (11¾ x 8½ in.)
Judith Rothschild Collection
(DC 151a)

92 *Head of a Harlequin, after Cézanne*,
1916
Pencil on paper
25.5 x 20.5 cm. (10 x 8⅛ in.)
Musée National d'Art Moderne,
Centre Georges Pompidou, Paris
[Washington only]

93 *Still Life with Knife*, 1917
Pencil on paper
26.7 x 38.1 cm. (10½ x 15 in.)
Thos. Marc Futter Collection

94 *Portrait of Madame Lipchitz*, 1918
Pencil on paper
47.5 x 30.5 cm. (18¾ x 12 in.)
Galerie Louise Leiris, Paris

95 *Study for "Harlequin with Guitar"*
(Study for "Seated Harlequin with Guitar"), 1919
Pen and ink on paper
29.8 x 22.9 cm. (11¾ x 9 in.)
Galerie Louise Leiris, Paris

96 *Still Life*, 1920
Pencil on paper
25 x 32.5 cm. (9¾ x 12¾ in.)
Private collection, Paris

97 *Portrait of Daniel-Henry Kahnweiler*,
1921
Pencil on paper
32.5 x 26 cm. (12¾ x 10¼ in.)
Private collection, Paris

98 *Portrait of Madame Louise Leiris*,
1921
Pencil on paper
34 x 26 cm. (13⅜ x 10¼ in.)
Private collection, Paris

99 *Self-portrait*, 1921
Pencil on paper
33 x 25 cm. (13 x 9⅞ in.)
Galerie Louise Leiris, Paris

University Art Museum
Board of Trustees

Acknowledgements

The organization of this exhibition has brought great pleasure, in part for new and strengthened personal associations. Private collectors generously showed me their treasures and shared their enthusiasm for the art of Gris. As usual, colleagues at other museums were extremely helpful in advancing the cause of the exhibition. I want, particularly, to thank Brenda Richardson, The Baltimore Museum of Art; Dr. Christian Geelhaar, Kunstmuseum Basel; Dr. Peter Krieger, Nationalgalerie, Berlin; Dr. Hans Christoph von Tavel, Kunstmuseum Bern; Thomas T. Solley, Indiana University Art Museum, Bloomington; Robert Buck, Albright-Knox Art Gallery, Buffalo; Dr. Seymor Slive and Ada Bordaloosa, Fogg Art Museum, Cambridge; James Wood, A. James Speyer, and Anne Rorimer, The Art Institute of Chicago; Dr. Hugo Borger, Museum Ludwig, Cologne; Budd Harris Bishop, Columbus Museum of Art; Homan Potterton, National Gallery of Ireland, Dublin; Dr. Werner Schmalenbach, Kunstsammlung Nordrhein-Westfalen, Düsseldorf; Rudi Fuchs and Magriet Suren, van Abbemuseum, Eindhoven; Tracy Atkinson and Gregory Hedberg, Wadsworth Atheneum, Hartford; Dr. Ole Henrik Moe and Karin Hellandsjo, Sonja Henie-Niels Onstad Foundations, Høvikodden; Federico Sopeña, Museo del Prado, Madrid; Samuel Sachs II, The Minneapolis Institute of Arts; Alan Shestack, Yale University Art Gallery, New Haven; Charles Chetham, Smith College Museum of Art, Northampton; Dr. R. W. O. Oxenaar, Mrs. Toos van Kooten, and J. B. J. Bremer, Rijksmuseum Kröller-Müller, Otterlo; Dominique Bozo, Henri de Cazals, and Germain Viatte, Musée National d'Art Moderne, Centre Georges Pompidou, Paris; Anne d'Harnoncourt, Philadelphia Museum of Art; Gerald D. Bolas, Washington University Gallery of Art, St. Louis; Paul D. Schweizer, Munson-Williams-Proctor Institute, Utica; Carl Belz, Rose Art Museum, Brandeis University, Waltham; Laughlin Phillips and Willem de Looper, The Phillips Collection, Washington, D.C.; Richard A. Madigan, Norton Gallery of Art, West Palm Beach. Colleagues at the museums on the tour of the exhibition have been gracious throughout the preparations. I am grateful to J. Carter Brown, E. A. Carmean, Jr., and Trinkett Clark at the National Gallery of Art in Washington, D.C., and Thomas M. Messer, Diane Waldman, Susan Hirschfeld, and Louise Svendsen at The Solomon R. Guggenheim Museum in New York.

Exhibitions are considerably aided by dealers who share in the appreciation of an artist. It has been a joy for me to work with Louise Leiris and her associate Maurice Jardot at the Galerie Leiris, Paris. Also of considerable help were Elvira Mignoni and her associate Soledad Lorenazo, Galeria Theo, Madrid. I also want to express my thanks to William Acquavella and Eleanore Saidenberg, art dealers in New York City.

Douglas Cooper has offered valuable counsel from the early planning stages of the exhibition. His catalogue raisonné of Gris's work is a magnificent achievement and was an invaluable tool in the research of the exhibition. Others who were most helpful include Alice Martin, National Endowment for the Arts; Heinz Berggruen, Paris; Bertha Saunders, curator of the David Rockefeller Collection; and Gary Tinterow, Harvard University.

I am grateful to Ron Johnson for his insightful comments on the manuscript, Ann Smock for her careful translations, Ann Karlstrom for her skilled editing, and Nathan Garland for his outstanding catalogue design.

On the staff of the Museum, two persons in particular have devoted enormous time and energy. Elise Goldstein has handled an impressive range of complex responsibilities with skill; her work on the chronology, bibliography, and exhibition history has been outstanding. Eve Vanderstoel has been a patient and essential force in making certain that great quantities of material were organized properly, accurately typed, and produced on deadline. Others on the staff who have devoted notable effort were Anne Aaboe, Business Manager; Jack Coyle, Registrar; Cathy Curtis, Editor; Ron Egherman, Assistant Director; Kit Livingston, formerly Development Director; Nina Hubbs, Designer; David Holbrook, Assistant Designer; David Ross, formerly Chief Curator; and Lesley Wright, Secretary to the Director. James Elliott, Director, has been involved with virtually every aspect of the exhibition.

The effort to organize an exhibition of this scale requires the continuous attention of a confidant. That person, as always, is Laura Rosenthal.

MR

Lenders to the Exhibition

The Baltimore Museum of Art

Kunstmuseum Basel

Staatliche Museen Preussischer Kulturbesitz, Nationalgalerie, Berlin

Kunstmuseum Bern

Indiana University Art Museum, Bloomington

Albright-Knox Art Gallery, Buffalo

Fogg Art Museum, Harvard University, Cambridge, Massachusetts

The Art Institute of Chicago

Museum Ludwig, Cologne

Columbus Museum of Art

National Gallery of Ireland, Dublin

Kunstsammlung Nordrhein-Westfalen, Düsseldorf

Van Abbemuseum, Eindhoven, Netherlands

Wadsworth Atheneum, Hartford, Connecticut

Sonja Henie-Niels Onstad Foundations, Høvikodden, Norway

Museo del Prado, Madrid

The Minneapolis Institute of Arts

Yale University Art Gallery, New Haven

The Solomon R. Guggenheim Museum, New York

Smith College Museum of Art, Northampton, Massachusetts

Rijksmuseum Kröller-Müller, Otterlo, Netherlands

Musée National d'Art Moderne, Centre Georges Pompidou, Paris

Philadelphia Museum of Art

Washington University Gallery of Art, Saint Louis, Missouri

Munson-Williams-Proctor Institute, Utica, New York

Rose Art Museum, Brandeis University, Waltham, Massachusetts

National Gallery of Art, Washington, D.C.

The Phillips Collection, Washington, D.C.

Norton Gallery of Art, West Palm Beach, Florida

Mr. and Mrs. James W. Alsdorf
The Colin Collection
Walter Feilchenfeldt
Mr. and Mrs. Roy J. Friedman
Thos. Marc Futter
Georges Gonzalez-Gris
Renée Gonzalez-Gris
Alex Hillman Family Foundation
M. Meyer
Mr. and Mrs. Morton G. Neumann
Judith Rothschild
Collection S
Stephen A. Simon and Bonnie Simon
Carlos Sobrino
Jerome H. Stone
James Johnson Sweeney
Mr. and Mrs. Burton Tremaine
Katherine Urquhart Warren
Rolf and Margit Weinberg
Richard S. Zeisler
Private collectors

Acquavella Galleries, Inc., New York
Davlyn Gallery, New York
Marisa del Re Gallery, New York
Galerie Jan Krugier, Geneva
Perls Galleries, New York
Saidenberg Gallery, New York
Galeria Theo, Madrid
Galerie Louise Leiris, Paris

Index

Photographic Credits

The photographs in this volume have been provided, in the majority of cases, by the owners or custodians of the works and are reproduced by their permission.

Copyright of certain works herein reproduced is controlled by S.P.A.D.E.M., Paris/V.A.G.A., New York, and as to such works the following notice is applicable: © VAGA/SPADEM 1983. In addition, the following photographic credits are noted:

Photoatelier Jörg P. Anders, Museum Dahlem, Berlin: 32
Lee Brian, Palm Beach: 45
Ken Cohen, New York: Fig. 7
A. C. Cooper Ltd., London: 47
Martien F. J. Coppens, Eindhoven: 64
Juan Dolcet, Madrid: 18, 63
Walter Dräyer, Zurich: 67, 84
Galerie Louise Leiris, Paris: 1, 2, 16, 39, 68, 69, 96, 97, 98, 99, Fig. 23, and
    all photographs reproduced in the Chronology unless otherwise indicated
Rolf Graber, Foto-Schopf, Muri, Switzerland: 81
Rodolphe Haller, Geneva: 5
Hans Hinz, Allschwill, Switzerland: Fig. 18
Jacqueline Hyde, Service de Documentation Photographique des Collections
    du Musée National d'Art Moderne, Paris: 37
Marie-Louise Jeanneret, Art Moderne, Geneva: Fig. 21
Bob Kolbrener, Saint Louis: 42
Robert E. Mates, New York: 4, 80
Joe Mikuliak, Philadelphia: 10
Daniel Mille, Monte Carlo: 7
Muldoon Studio, Waltham, Massachusetts: 14
The Museum of Modern Art, New York: Fig. 8
Nationalmuseum Stockholm: 74
Eric Pollitzer, New York: 44, 53
Service de Documentation Photographique de la Réunion des Musées Nationaux,
    Paris: 75, 92, Fig. 22
Steiner + Co. AG, Basel: 11
Ken Strothman and Harvey Osterhoudt, Indiana University Art Museum,
    Bloomington: 87
Joseph Szaszfai, Branford, Connecticut: 40, Fig. 17
Michael Tropea, Chicago: 9, 58, 61
Malcolm Varon, New York: 20, 23, 70
Sharon White, Waltham, Massachusetts: 83

Juan